The Good , the Bad , and the Ugly

A Readers' and Writers' Guide for Believers

by

Michael J. and Mary C. Findley

Findley Family Video Publications

The Good , the Bad , and the Ugly: A Readers' and Writers' Guide for Believers

by Michael J. and Mary C. Findley

"Speaking the truth in love."

Table of Contents

Appendix
(Findley Family Video Technical and Content Standards)

Other Products from Findley Family Video

Introduction

Are There Standards?

The short answer is yes. Of course. We live in a world where we are taught that everything is relative, nothing is black and white, and nobody can tell you what you can and can't do. But you still can't pop open a tank of sulfuric acid and breathe it instead of air. Your neighbor's living room is still not a parking place for your car. We do still sometimes manage to execute murderers.

The problem is that people fundamentally confuse liberty with license. They think that there should be as few rules in life as possible, perhaps only ones that relate to banishing ignorance, protecting personal property, and ensuring safety.

Certainly standards should not be applied to the written word. We are long past the horrors of censorship, aren't we? The U.S. Constitution protects the Freedom of the Press, and that's kind of a worldwide standard, that only repressive governments tell people what they can and can't (or should and shouldn't) read.

What if a book had such exemplary, uplifting, beautiful content that everyone would be refreshed and encouraged and made better just by reading it? Who would not spread the word that between those covers lies an elixir of life? Who would not be outraged if it were forbidden to share such good news?

But what if a piece of writing could affect someone just like a deadly poison? Who wouldn't at least put a warning label on it? You may have even heard the term "poison pen," referring to writing designed to destroy opposition. In a mental, emotional, and spiritual sense, writing can be poison, whether people believe it or not. Is it a suppression of the writer's freedom to add a warning to such a work, that its purpose is destructive and potentially deadly?

Oh, *those* standards. Well, those would be okay, as long as they are completely accurate, fair, and objective, and they don't stomp on anybody's freedom or hurt anybody's feelings.

In other words, no, there can't be any standards, because human beings *have* no such perfect standards. There is nothing everyone agrees on.

> *The sign of a natural law must be the universal respect in which it is held ... we would undoubtedly obey it universally ... Instead there is nothing in the world that is not subject to contradiction and dispute ... there is nothing that is strange and unnatural that is not approved in many countries ...Pierre Charron, from de Sagasse*

Let's just take one word as an example. We're writing the book, so we get to pick the word. But we think it's an excellent word for our purposes, since we are talking about standards in writing, and potentially, the ability to make decisions about what to read and write and how to advise others along these lines. Here is the word:

Choice

Let's define the word choice. Various dictionaries will provide not only meaning, but etymology (word origin), and examples of usage, sometimes throughout history, showing how the word might have changed in meaning. Following is one dictionary's listing for this word, chosen at random.

Choice

noun

1. an act of selecting or making a decision when faced with two or more possibilities. "the choice between good and evil"

Synonyms: option, alternative, possible course of action "you have no other choice"

the right or ability to make, or possibility of making, such a selection. "I had to do it, I had no choice"

Synonyms: selection, election, choosing, picking; a range of possibilities from which one or more may be selected. "you can have a sofa made to order in a choice of over forty fabrics"

Synonyms: selection, election, choosing, picking; a course of action, thing, or person that is selected or decided upon. "this CD drive is the perfect choice for your computer"

Synonyms: preference, selection, pick, favorite

adjective

adjective: choice; comparative adjective: choicer; superlative adjective: choicest

1. (especially of food) of very good quality.

"he picked some choice early plums"

Synonyms: superior, first-class, first-rate, prime, premier, grade A, best, finest, excellent, select, quality, high-quality, top, top-quality, high-grade, prize, fine, special

Antonyms: inferior

2. (of words, phrases, or language) rude and abusive.

"he had a few choice words at his command"

Wow, did you know that word had so many nuances of meaning? Maybe you didn't think about it beforehand, but you've had your "Oh, yeah" moment now, and you see the possibilities in the word *choice,* right?

Recently We have been following a story many around the world may know nothing about. In the country of Sudan, there is a woman whose father is a Muslim and her mother is a Christian. The father seems to have abandoned the family. The daughter was raised by her mother as a Christian, married a Christian man, already has one small child, and was pregnant with a second.

This woman was arrested and jailed, and her young child along with her. She was sentenced to 100 lashes and hanging. The compassionate government did promise to give her a reprieve until the birth of her second child.

What was her crime? The government says she made a wrong *choice*. She chose to practice Christianity, the religion of her mother, instead of Islam, the religion of her father (who abandoned the family). In Islamic Sudan, Christian marriages are not recognized, so she is accused of adultery. For that, she has been shackled in a prison cell, and her small child is there in also, and she has given birth there. And the sentence is still 100 lashes and execution by hanging. Did you know that the word *choice* meant all that? (Meriam Ibrahim, the woman in this story, has since been permitted to leave the country in safety with her husband.)

You might feel outrage over this. You might cry foul, and demand that the woman and her children go free. But her government has said she had a choice that could have prevented all this. It was her decision that led to these horrifying circumstances, and she has to bear those consequences.

Consider this also. A child, one with a beating heart, ten fingers, ten toes, not significantly different from any child you see anywhere in the world, just a few months younger than most, can, depending on the locale, have his beating heart stilled, his tiny spine snapped with a pair of scissors, his place of safety and comfort flooded with poison, his limbs chopped up like so much kindling, and all that is also a definition of the word *choice*. Not the child's choice, certainly, but the choice of his own mother.

In this case, it is nearly impossible to make the people who favor this choice even listen to a description of this child's fate. You can be arrested just for talking to a mother entering an abortion clinic. You will be verbally attacked, lied about, and accused of assault just for trying to save that tiny life, to change that deadly choice with consequences reaching far beyond that one decision.

Go back to the definition of the word choice above and read again the first example of the word's usage. Here it is, in case you don't bother: "the choice between good and evil." Remember, this is a definition picked at random, based on a Google search. We didn't even know what dictionary it came from at the time we picked it out.

Maybe you don't believe in good and evil. Maybe you think they are antiquated words we need not pay attention to. But those words are still in the dictionary, just like the word choice. If you look them up at random, the definitions might surprise you, might give you an "oh, yeah" moment. They might also be incomplete, like the one for choice.

In our book the *Conflict of the Ages Part Two: The Origin of Evil in the World That Was*, we make a statement about good. God is the origin of good. At the end of Creation, God states that everything "was very good." We also make two statements in that book about evil. One is that God is not the author or originator of evil. The other is that evil originated with Satan.

Here, then, are the world's first standards, and here is our first and most fundamental choice. Good comes from God, and evil comes from Satan. Time to make a choice. Choose good, or choose evil. Do it right now, and keep on doing it, every second, minute, hour, all your life. Oh, by the way, your choices likely have lifelong, pervasive, and even eternal consequences.

You may smugly reply, "There are plenty of choices that aren't good or evil. Chocolate or vanilla ice cream, for example." Maybe that's true, but you know as well as we do that many, if not most, choices have consequences; good consequences or evil ones. Maybe the consequences are just a little good or a little evil. Maybe there are gigantic amounts such as spillover into other people's lives; maybe life-changing fallout for you, for the entire world, for everybody's future.

"Wait!" You exclaim. "This isn't fair! All my life I've been told choice is freedom. How can I even *tell* what's good and what's evil?"

We're glad you asked.

Why Does It Matter?

Or, maybe you didn't ask. But if you haven't just tossed this book aside, like it or not, you accept that good and evil exist, and that they are the reason we need standards. The subject of good and evil, of course, encompasses much more than just what to read or not read, or what to recommend or warn against. And no frail, finite human can just make good choices or give good advice or set good standards all his life on his own.

Remember that good comes from God. To learn what something is and how to make use of it, your best bet is to consult the creator. Happily, the Creator of good also wrote down His own set of standards. It is called the Holy Scriptures.

Simply stated, standards matter because our choices help or harm us. They make us better or worse. To use the supposedly neutral example above, chocolate ice cream could produce an allergic reaction and result in a trip to the ER or a shot from an Epipen. It could have more calories than vanilla, and cost us a few more pounds of weight gain. It could stain a favorite shirt, where vanilla might wash out more easily. These aren't overtly good and evil consequences, but if you let your thinking drift out of the physical realm and into the spiritual realm, it's not so hard to imagine comparable consequences for actions that are choices between good or evil.

So it matters because little by little, inch by inch, step by step, our choices move us in a direction. That one was good. Yay! Oops. That one was bad. Boo. Good one. Good one. Good one. Oops. Bad one. Do you want to live your life like a rabbit, hopping from safety to supper with no way of knowing what the next hop will bring?

Even rabbits have standards. They have ears, noses, and eyes that can give them hints of danger or good eating. Experts tell us they can even judge how soil falls in a burrow and make decisions about whether it's safe to keep digging or time to get out. These decisions, based on these standards, are health and safety, life and death, to a rabbit. How can humans possibly think standards are optional?

So, in the mental, emotional, and spiritual realms, our choices can also make or break us. They can form good or bad habits and step us along a path toward or away from what is good for us. Standards are kind of like a plan. We need one, or we won't make very good choices. The question is, where do we get that plan?

I'm glad you asked.

Who Made You Judge?

Or, maybe you didn't ask. But you still didn't toss the book, so we will tell you that God made us fruit inspectors. He made you one too. We can't see into the heart. God told Samuel this as he was choosing Israel's second king, who turned out to be David.

> *But the LORD said unto Samuel, Look not on his countenance, or on the height of his stature; because I have refused him: for the LORD seeth not as man seeth; for man looketh on the outward appearance, but the LORD looketh on the heart.*
> I Samuel 16:7

So even though we can't be positive about what is in a person's heart, we can check out his fruit. The Bible talks a lot about being a fruit inspector, so let's just cut to the chase and see the future of the bad fruit producer.

> *The axe is already laid at the root of the trees; therefore every tree that does not bear good fruit is cut down and thrown into the fire.* (Matthew 3:9)

So, shifting this out of the earthly realm and into the spiritual one, and more particularly, into our standards for writing discussion, the tree is the writer, the fruit is his writing, and the ax is the standard. We are not the ones who are going to cut that guy (not just his writing) off and toss him into the flames. We didn't make the ax. God did.

This is why it matters. There are eternal consequences for making good or evil choices. God already knows the good from the evil. He already forged the ax. Right now we can just apply standards to writing and help avoid future physical and spiritual consequences to actual people. We have to do whatever we can to spare people those eternal consequences by showing them the truth about good and evil; by cutting down the bad authors with their evil fruit and tossing those things into the fire.

Is that unfair? Is that cruel? Are you calling God names, like so many popular secularists, saying He's a "bloody bully" and we've grown beyond using His standard, His ax, to purge evil? These days, it's live and let live, and forget God because He is just out to knock us down, subjugate us, and rob us of hope.

We'll give you the truth in three different translations, so there's no mistake about what God really is, and does, and means by His actions toward us.

Jeremiah 29:11

"For I know the plans that I have for you," declares the Lord, "plans for welfare and not for calamity to give you a future and a hope." (NASB)

"For I know the thoughts that I think toward you," saith the Lord, "thoughts of peace, and not of evil, to give you an expected end." (KJV)

"For I know the plans that I have for you," declares the LORD, "plans for well-being, and not for calamity, in order to give you a future and a hope." (ISV)

Get it? He's got plans, and they're good ones, plans for peace, for hope, not for evil.

Think blueprints. If you build a building just any old way, the roof will leak, steps will drop off in the middle of the stairwell, doors will open into solid walls. God knows how thing have to work. He has the blueprints. He has the standards. Let's go dig some out.

Please note that in this book the first section will take, for the most part, a "perfect politician" stand. Most people have said, "I wish that candidate would stop telling us what's wrong with his opponent and start telling us what's right about himself!" So the focus in the beginning will be to point out what's good about books, and what to look for, more than what to avoid. There will be some guidelines about what to avoid there, and also in later sections. But remember classic bank teller training to spot counterfeit bills consisted of only handling real bills. After passing thousands of good bills through your fingers, you too should be pretty good at feeling a fake one. Times have changed, of course, and so has teller training, but focusing on what makes something good is still the best way to learn good. It's better than wallowing in the mudhole where evil lives. Let's keep as clean as we can, shall we?

> *Finally, brethren, whatsoever things are true, whatsoever things are honest, whatsoever things are just, whatsoever things are pure, whatsoever things are lovely, whatsoever things are of good report; if there be any virtue, and if there be any praise, think on these things.* (Philippians 4:8)

Section One: Recognizing the Good Writing

(from the Book of Philippians)

Chapter One: Thankful, Prayerful, Joyful

It is possible to teach standards by which to judge writing from anywhere in the Bible. In fact, it might be good to go through the entire Scriptures and mine them for writing standards. However, for the sake of focus, We chose to base this first section of the book on Philippians, jumping off from Chapter Four, verse eight, quoted above at the end of the introduction.

Philippians Chapter One sets the bar pretty high for the audience. It calls them saints, which includes all believers. One translation even calls them "holy ones." (ISV) *Wow.* So we know from the start that the unconverted can't really hope to follow standards taught in the Word of God. Their minds aren't tuned to listen to God. They aren't washed from their filthiness. The first thing you need, therefore, is to be a believer in Christ. The second thing is to be able to recognize Christlikeness in what you read.

Thankful

First, seek out writers who know how to be thankful, and especially thankful for God's grace and peace. Look for the ways they write about how they identify it in other believers. Paul thanked God for and experienced joy over his spiritual children. He saw the work that God had begun in them and knew that it would keep growing to perfection.

Fellowship in Growth

We all need to be growing in Christ as believers, and what we read needs to encourage that fellowship in growth. Gardeners sometimes get together and talk about what works and what doesn't when they grow plants. Their focus is on making the plants grow better. They might have to talk about infestations or diseases or unhealthy conditions, but their focus is swapping notes on the right food, the right soil, the right protection to prevent sick or dead plants. In the same way, you can recognize a good writer by his ratio of stuff that lifts you up versus stuff that knocks you down.

Defense of Truth
Can you be thankful that you read that book because the writer defends truth? Paul urges his readers to understand that love is based on "real knowledge and discernment" (Philippians 1:9, NASB). He said that was the only way they could "approve the things that are excellent" and be "sincere and blameless" (v. 10, NASB) as well as "filled with the fruit of righteousness" (v. 11, NASB). This fruitful tree is the polar opposite of the one in Matthew 3:9, which we talked about in the introduction. Far from producing evil fruit, this one has a bumper crop of righteousness. Don't you want to read a book that's filled with righteousness?

Confirmation of Witness
Is the writer a confirming witness? Paul said his imprisonment, far from being a bad thing, had turned out "for the greater progress of the Gospel" (v. 12). People who saw Paul make Christ known to "the whole praetorian guard and to everyone else" took their courage in hand and started confirming Paul's witness.

Partnership in Persecution
It made him especially happy when the Gospel was preached by those who demonstrated their love and support for Paul by echoing his message. They became partners in Paul's persecution. "For to you it has been granted for Christ's sake, not only to believe in Him, but also to suffer for His sake" (v. 29). Those are the authors where we can find real focus for our reading choices. Paul was ready to live or die for Christ, and he praised

those who were "in no way alarmed by your opponents" (v. 28). The Scriptures say persecution will come on believers, and it is everywhere today. Seek out people who are not afraid to partner with the persecuted and share the message of truth.

Regardless of Motivation

Paul even took joy in people who preached the Gospel for the wrong reasons. Some writers seem to have an envious spirit, copying the message to try to get personal gain out of it. Instead of despising the televangelist, be aware of what truth there is in his message. We have to condemn heresy but Paul said that even people who might be trying to add to his burden of imprisonment made him happy, as long as the Gospel was preached.

Prayerful

Not only should we gravitate toward thankful writers, but let's also look for those who are prayerful. That doesn't mean we should go looking for prayer books to read, although prayer books can be great reading. The Scriptures tell us to *pray without ceasing* (I Thessalonians 5:17). Look for writers who evidence an attitude of prayer. What are some prayerful characteristics in writing?

For Compassion

First, look for compassion. Paul said he had these believers *in his heart* (v. 7) and also said, *how I long for you all with the affection of Christ Jesus* (v. 8). He showed compassion for those who guarded him by sharing the Gospel with them. You can also look for a writer who encourages others to show compassion, and reminds us that God calls us to *admonish the unruly, encourage the fainthearted, help the weak, be patient with everyone.* (1 Thessalonians 5:14 ISV).

For Growth

Find a writer whose heart clearly wants people to grow in Christ.

> *"The only thing that matters is that you continue to live as good citizens in a manner worthy of the gospel of the Messiah. Then, whether I come to see you or whether I stay away, I may hear all about you—that you are standing firm in one spirit, struggling with one mind for the faith of the gospel"* (v 27 ISV).

He wants them to be worthy, to stand firm, to be of one mind. He doesn't want them to feel sorry for him because he is in prison. He wants them to be bold, like he is, communicating the message to his "captive audience" of Roman guards, and they follow his example. Paul shows an example of how to grow.

For Discernment

A good writer communicates the need for discernment. *So that you may be able to choose what is best and be pure and blameless until the day when the Messiah returns* (Philippians 1:10). Just being able to tell the difference between the preachers who speak out of jealousy and to cause rifts and those who do it because they love Paul and Christ is a strong example. Today we are told to love and accept everyone who names the name of Christ. The Scriptures, however, point out that not all who name the name of Christ should be accepted or followed.

> *"Many will say to me on that day, 'Lord, Lord, we prophesied in your name, drove out demons in your name, and performed many miracles in your name, didn't we?' Then I will tell them plainly, 'I never knew you. Get away from me, you who practice evil!'"* (Matthew 7:22, 23 ISV)

Once again, there is a flip side to this. Jesus Christ Himself explained that people can do His work without being obviously one of his followers.

> *John told Jesus, "Teacher, we saw someone driving out demons in your name. We tried to stop him, because he wasn't a follower like us." But Jesus said, "Don't stop him, because no one who works a miracle in my name can slander me soon afterwards. Whoever is not against us is for us. I tell you with certainty, whoever gives you a cup of water to drink because you belong to the Messiah will never lose his reward."* (Mark 9:38-41 ISV)

Remember the incident in Acts where men tried to cast out demons in Jesus' name?

> *Then some Jews who went around trying to drive out demons attempted to use the name of the Lord Jesus on those who had evil spirits, saying, "I command you by that Jesus whom Paul preaches!" Seven sons of a Jewish high priest named Sceva were doing this. But the evil spirit told them, "Jesus I know, and I am getting acquainted with Paul, but who are you?" Then the man with the evil spirit jumped on them, got the better of them, and so violently overpowered all of them that they fled out of the house naked and bruised. When this became known to everyone living in Ephesus, Jews and Greeks alike, they all became terrified, and the name of the Lord Jesus began to be held in high honor.* (Acts 19:13-17 ISV)

So here is a mini-lesson in discernment. 1. Jesus alone knows people's hearts, so He has the final say about those who are truly His and can and does reject those who are not. Pray and study the Scriptures to get better acquainted with the mind of Christ. (Matthew 7:22-23)

2. The people the disciples tried to rebuke were not doing evil because Jesus said those who do a miracle in His name, or even something as small as giving a drink to a follower of Christ, can't turn around and do evil. (Mark 9:38-41) 3. People who try to use Christ's name but fail are not of God. Don't forget, however, that the good outcome of glory to God (*the name of the Lord Jesus began to be held in high honor)* can still come from these people who falsely name the name of Christ. (Acts 19:13-17)

For Unity

We keep flipping coins around here, so flip it again. Do not major on minors to cause division. *Standing firm in one spirit ... struggling with one mind...* (v. 27 ISV) Remember we are in a partnership, not permitting compromise, but fostering unity. People who drive wedges into the fellowship of believers are often not true members of the Body of Christ. *They went out from us, but they were not really of us; for if they had been of us, they would have remained with us; but they went out, so that it would be shown that they all are not of us* (1 John 2:19 ISV).

Remember the key from Philippians 1:1: *who are in union with the Messiah Jesus,* united with other believers and one with Jesus Christ. Paul's statement about being *partners with me in this privilege* reminds us that unity means we get to be a part of a glorious ministry. Look for books that reveal a biblical partnership and ministry, and don't waste time quibbling over whether the work is done exactly as you would do it. Don't read about or be the one guilty of that *jealousy and dissension.* (v. 15) Be the one who can say, *the Messiah is being proclaimed. Because of this, I rejoice and will continue to rejoice.*

For Deliverance

In Paul's case, two kinds of deliverance were possible: release from prison or death and freedom in Heaven with Christ. Just because a book doesn't have a happy ending where prisoners go physically free doesn't mean it isn't a good book. The Scriptures say, *If we have set our hopes on the Messiah in this life only, we deserve more pity than any other people* (I Corinthians 15:19 ISV).

The context in this chapter is that the Gospel is the death, burial, and resurrection of Christ, but Paul also taught that we have a future, eternal hope, not just hope in this life. Millions have been imprisoned, kidnapped, tortured, had their possessions stolen, their means to make a living denied, and their whole lives made miserable because of faith in Christ. Paul suffered these same torments off and on throughout his life. Sometimes this life will never get good, in the human comfort sense, for some people. The closer you are to Christ, the less likely your life is to be peaceful.

I know that this will result in my deliverance through your prayers and the help that comes from the Spirit of Jesus the Messiah says Paul in v. 19. But keep reading. In v. 20 he says, *whether I live or die.* In v. 21 he says, *For to me, to go on living is the Messiah, and to die is gain.* He says that leaving this life means being with the Messiah, *which is far better.* But he explains that he is convinced it is better for the believers if he stays alive for now, so he believes that he will be physically delivered from prison for now.

Does that book you are reading even mention that dying and going to heaven is better than staying in this life? Does it say that if you do live, you live only for Christ? Or does it focus on the here and now, on material things, on how to be comfortable and live well and succeed in an earthly sense? We don't think Paul spent a lot of time reading or recommending those kinds of books. We don't think Jesus did either. *Love not the world, neither the things that are in the world,* says I John 2:15 ISV.

Books that remind you to pray for and do whatever you can to comfort, encourage, and help the persecuted church should definitely be on your "to-read" list. It's not unrealistic to pray for or write about physical deliverance for those people. Just because the Scriptures say that *in this life we shall have persecution* (I Thessalonians 3:4) doesn't mean we shouldn't share encouragement about the possibility of physical freedom for these believers.

For Encouragement

Then your rejoicing in the Messiah Jesus will increase along with mine when I visit with you again. (Philippians 1:26 ISV) Stories about the encouragement of fellow believers are a must for the to-read list. Those who devote their lives to teaching and building up believers are great subjects for writing. Such teachers are themselves encouraged when those they minister to show evidence of growth. Stories where characters refuse to let opponents hinder their work are encouraging also. (v. 28) The knowledge that enemies will be destroyed and believers saved is very heartening. Even though the Scriptures say to love your enemies, they also say, *Vengeance is mine, I will repay, saith the Lord.* (Romans 12:19) God at times encourages His people by judging their enemies.

Joyful

I rejoice because I eagerly expect and hope that I will have nothing to be ashamed of, says Paul in Philippians 1:20. We read a lot of reviews of books that throw out the words "joyous" or "full of joy", but I think people often confuse the word *joy* with the word happy, and that they are looking for some giddy feeling with no real basis. Perhaps they want satisfaction or good feelings from personal victories, or from making the world a better place. Paul sets joy in opposition to shame. He challenges us to consider rejoicing is not always being happy but being unashamed.

Assured

Will Jesus Christ be exalted in your life? Do you know that for sure? How about in your death? Paul had this assurance. He knew it for a fact. If there was a book that taught you how to be that Christ-exalting person, living or dead, wouldn't you want to read it? What a wonderful book is the one that leaves you stronger Christ, more determined to glorify Him.

Aware

Imagine knowing that as long as you go on living, your work will have eternal value. We have heard many people, as Father's Day approaches each year, ask what good things fathers teach us. A common answer is "the value of hard work." Books should teach us this too, and not just in the physical sense. Look for books that teach you about the need to work for Christ. Prayerfully read ones that teach you how to work *hard* for Christ. Paul was aware of the importance of this work. He was also eager to make others aware of it, and to help them see that it could produce joy.*I know that I will continue to live and be with all of you, so you will mature in the faith and know joy in it.* (v. 25)

A certain former president and his wife still talk about how hard he worked, how hard they worked, for the American people. But many do not see their work as for our good at all, and many honestly hope it does *not* have eternal consequences. What you read should make you aware of whether what you are doing has real value for eternity and for the cause of Christ.

Bold

Nobody defines boldness quite like the Apostle Paul, though he said he was *the least of all the apostles*. How do we become bold like Paul? More importantly, what does being bold have to do with being joyful? Paul was bold enough to witness to prison guards. He didn't stop until he could say with certainty that the whole praetorian guard had heard the truth of Christ. And he wasn't saying it to brag. He was expressing his joy that so many had heard. Paul's goal if/when he got out of prison was to continue overseeing believers' progress *so you will mature in the faith and know joy in it.*

Peter Pan didn't want to grow up. He didn't think it would be any fun. But Wendy found joy in becoming a wife and mother; in maturing. Paul was confident that believers would find the same joy as they "grew up." *Then your rejoicing in the Messiah Jesus will increase along with mine when I visit with you again.* (v. 26) Books that produce rejoicing in Christ, and increase it, are great books.

Confident

People sometimes complain that a book is too predictable; that there are no surprises and it is boring. But it's a good thing for a book to give you confidence in its message. You should be convinced, as Paul was in v. 1:28, that the good guys will win and the bad guys will lose. *And that you are not intimidated by your opponents in any way. This is evidence that they will be destroyed and that you will be saved—and all because of God.* It's not that the good guys will have an easy time of it, but that they will be confident, not intimidated, in the face of the enemy.

Expectant

A book should make you love and look for the Lord's appearing, or your approaching time to go to be with Him. *Now when these things begin to take place, stand up and lift up your heads, because your deliverance is approaching.* (Luke 21:28) In the preceding verses Jesus talks about times of great trouble, possibly the end times. He lists some signs, and some very bad things that will happen to His followers. Many people will react with terror and hopelessness. Believers, however, should realize that Christ is coming. The worse things get, the more likely it is that His coming is at hand. We will suffer persecution, the world will get worse and worse, and there is little hope of peace, happiness, or safety for the believer in this world. Paul acknowledged that there were two ways to meet Christ – by his return, and by death. Books that make you expectant (not fearful, angry, or indifferent) about either outcome are good ones.

Fearless

Do you sometimes worry, when people you know are going to see you for the first time in a long time? Have you put on some weight? Will they be disappointed in you in some way? Paul was confident that he was coming to see the believers at Philippi, or at least that he would hear all about them. Were they worried about how he would find them?

We need to read books that prepare us to meet more mature saints. Paul mentions many things he looks for in his spiritual children, and these qualities should be reinforced in our reading. *Continue to live ... worthy* is our charge. *Stand firm,* have *faith in the Gospel,* don't be intimidated, and count it a privilege to serve Him and to suffer for Him. Books that teach us these kinds of preparation will ready us to be fearless before our spiritual elders, and before our Savior Himself.

Fruitful

Paul insisted that his continued life would result in fruitful service. It's not automatic that people who accept Christ will become fruitful. It requires study, discipline, and growth. And remember that fruitful doesn't necessarily mean that you witness to thousands of people and seen them accept Jesus. In the early church some numbers were given of how many people joined the church, but that didn't continue long. Remember that *the fruit of the Spirit is love, joy, peace, patience, kindness, goodness, faithfulness, gentleness, self-control; against such things there is no law* (Galatians 5:22-23). Books need to show that people who are fruitful are producing fruit within themselves, and that people who "pray the prayer" for salvation are genuine fruit-producers too.

Chapter Two: Humility, Service, and Sacrifice

Humility

It's strange to think of humility as having anything to do with encouragement. But look at the response of Moses in almost every hardship the children of Israel put him through. *Now the man Moses was very humble, more than any man who was on the face of the earth* (Numbers 12:3). The children of Israel were like surly teenagers. "Who said you were in charge?" "I'm dying of thirst!" "This is all your fault!" "There's nothing good to eat!" "Dad's not here, so let's party!" How did Moses respond? He cried out to God. He fell on his face. He prayed. And sometimes, he prayed that the people wouldn't be incinerated, and that God wouldn't make a new chosen people from Moses alone. That is humility. We am not saying he didn't experience anger, frustration, or any of the rest of the reasonable responses. But he cared about God's people and God's holiness more than his own comfort or advancement.

Encouragement

> *Therefore, if there is any encouragement in the Messiah, if there is any comfort of love, if there is any fellowship in the Spirit, if there is any compassion and sympathy, then fill me with joy by having the same attitude, sharing the same love, being united in spirit, and keeping one purpose in mind.* (Philippians 2:1)

One of the essential things books should do is be an encouragement, not a discouragement. That doesn't mean puff us up with artificial feelings of happiness or false praise when we should be slapped upside the head and told to get busy for God. It means that it should show us what's possible in Christ. No matter how difficult the world becomes, we need to be able to find books that can minister to us and lift us up.

Love

Philippians Two is stuffed with advice about how to show love in ways you might not have considered. Look for these in books you choose. Does your reading teach you how to do at least some of these things? Books also shouldn't avoid some "do nots." They should tell you not to be selfish, not to be conceited. Humility means considering others more important than yourself, just as Moses did after he got over the initial reaction of, (our paraphrase) "Did I give birth to all these people? Why do I have to carry them around like screaming babies?" Yes, Moses wasn't perfect. We can find books with imperfect people who "get over themselves" and then show us the right example.

Fellowship

Find books that include how to be company to those who share the Holy Spirit. Learn through your reading to be that one who fills your fellow believers, and also your spiritual leaders, with joy. Show them your godly attitude, a reflection of their teaching. They can see that your spirit is one with theirs. You all have one purpose. "What a fellowship, what a joy divine, leaning on the everlasting arms."

Sympathy

You know how lonely it is when you are surrounded by unbelievers who only know how say "good luck," or "thinking good thoughts," or "sending positive energy your way." Learn through your reading to have true compassion. Show real sympathy. Offer genuine comfort.

Service

There is no better example of selfless service than Jesus Christ. Philippians 2: 5-11 spells out the characteristics of the perfect hero. Heroes in books ought to exemplify, or change to become, this heroic character.

Abandon position

Kings step down from their thrones. Politicians leave office. Not just to become hermits, or to abandon responsibility. They take on a greater mission. Jesus Christ left heaven to teach, to heal, to love, and most of all, to be *tempted in all points like as we are*. We can't say He doesn't understand. Books can't say God is distant, unknowing, uncaring. Jesus Christ was here. He was one of us.

Embrace obedience

Disobedience "for a good cause" is a huge theme in literature. But Christ, and good books that emulate His example, show that obedience is for everyone. Find examples in books of people who obey when it's hard, when it doesn't seem to make sense, when you want to beg God to *let this cup pass from me*. Be able to absorb the example of *nevertheless, not my will* from what you read.

Exemplify salvation

How do we experience salvation? By hearing the Gospel. What is the Gospel? *The Messiah died for our sins according to the Scriptures, he was buried, he was raised on the third day according to the Scriptures—and is still alive!—* (I Corinthians 15: 3-4) How can a book *exemplify* salvation, and therefore be good reading material for us? It must include the whole salvation story. Not the easy-believism the world teaches. It must teach Christ's atonement, His cleansing blood, and His resurrection. Too many so-called Christians want to write what's popular, so they neglect to make clear that sin must be atoned for, and that Christ is our hope for now and for eternity.

Don't forget that the end of the "story" of Christ's servanthood and provision of salvation is his exaltation as King of Kings and Lord of Lords. The books you read should not make Him some "surfer dude" buddy. They should treat Him as holy and as Lord.

Sacrifice

Books today tend to dwell on making the reader feel special, unique, destined for greatness, through these things coming to pass for the main character. This is the opposite of the Scriptural example of dying to self. Even if the book includes a "happily ever after" of marrying the prince or ascending to the throne, the correct perspective is to be humbled and grateful for the love, the trust, or the prosperity that comes through "fulfilled destiny."

Submit to God

Just as you have always obeyed is not natural to man, but it had better be natural to you, and present in the books you read. Don't listen to the culture's cry "believe in yourself" or "listen to your heart." *The heart is deceitful above all things and desperately wicked. Who can know it?* (Jeremiah 17:9) This very book has said it before. Only God knows your heart. It has to be submitted to Him before it can be cleansed of its evil and made fit. You have to give up self. *It is God who is producing in you both the desire and the ability to do what pleases him.* (2:13)

Cease to complain

"Life isn't fair" is another theme books often rant about. *Do everything without complaining or arguing so that you may be blameless and innocent.* (2:14) This is the attitude you should look for in what you read. Complaining is sin. Having an "attitude," meaning to consistently respond to people with ill-temper, sarcasm, insults, arrogance, and impatience, is also now considered desirable in a "hero." Though this is not always sin, it is more characteristic of what used to be called an "anti-hero." Such character traits are not compatible with this teaching: *with humility think of others as being better than yourselves. Do not be concerned about your own interests, but also be concerned about the interests of others.* (2:3-4) This is the kind of hero to read about and take as an example.

Shine in purity

So that you may be blameless and innocent, God's children without any faults among a crooked and perverse generation, among whom you shine like stars in the world as you hold firmly to the word of life. (Philippians 2: 15-16)

How many books have you read with characters like these? It doesn't mean never having sinned. Paul could not say that about himself. He was a persecutor of the church. But he said, *Christ Jesus died to save sinners, of whom I am chief.* (1 Timothy 1:15) The way to shine in purity is to hold firmly to the Word of Life, the Scriptures. The blood of Jesus Christ, God's son, cleanses us from *all* sin.

Reflect on instruction

In fiction and nonfiction, many people say they had to rebel against their parents, teachers, employers. It is presented as a quest for freedom, usually. Sometimes there are bad authority figures in a person's life, but it is good to look for opportunities to honor those who raised you, instructed you, and gave you life experience. It is good to remember what they taught you. George Bailey, as a young man in the movie *It's a Wonderful Life,* wanted to be free, to "shake off the dust of this crummy little town," but, in reality, he remembered the teaching and example of his father, and poured his life into Bedford Falls just as his father had.

Pour out tirelessly

Paul was not the only person who gave everything for the cause of Christ. Timothy was Paul's son in the faith. Paul says he took a genuine interest in the Philippians' welfare. *For all the others look after their own interests, not after those of Jesus the Messiah. But you know his proven worth–how like a son with his father he served with me in the gospel* (Philippians 2:-22).

Epaphroditus nearly died in the service of Christ. It is interesting that he became ill *for the work of the Messiah by risking his life to complete what remained unfinished in your service to me.* This is a worthy sacrifice, and something your reading material ought to include. Not only did he sacrifice for Christ, but he endangered his health to fill in a gap left by those who may not have been able or willing to serve.

Chapter Three: Counterfeiters, Imitators, and Enemies

Philippians Three has a strange statement at the beginning. *So then, my brothers, keep on rejoicing in the Lord. It is no trouble for me to write the same things to you; indeed, it is for your safety.* (3:1) You may think some things in this book are repetitive, but as Paul says, repetition aids safety. You can't tell people too many times to keep rejoicing in the Lord. How is it for your safety? Several translations mention the idea of safety, but one says it is "necessary." Apparently good writers repeat things for our own good.

Counterfeiters

Paul not only wants to remind us to keep rejoicing, but he also wants us to remember to be on guard against false teaching. We mentioned counterfeiting in the introduction. We wish we could just avoid counterfeit Christians, but they are all around us. They also write books, so we need to watch out for them in what we read.

Dogs

In the Jewish culture, dogs are unclean. So perhaps Paul, when speaking about dogs, may have meant that we are not to accept what is unclean. Peter had a vision before preaching to Cornelius in which God showed him not to call anything common or unclean, and he had to learn that lesson more than once. Paul accused him publicly of wrongdoing when he separated from Gentiles to gain favor with visiting Jews. Peter was not to treat non-Jews earnestly seeking truth any differently from his fellow Israelites.

This is not what Paul is talking about here. He does not want people to pollute the church by inviting in those who are not cleansed from sin. Some people think we must show love for all by including everyone, regardless of whether their message is true.

Some believers participate in ecumenical meetings where people who do not believe the Scriptures and who teach heresy are allowed equal participation. We cannot love everyone so much that we allow them to cause confusion at best and corruption at worst in our churches. We should not be sucked in to believing error and watering down the word by what we read, either.

Evil workers

Those who put human, or even spiritual, experiences above the Word of God are evil workers. The Old Testament Scriptures warned against believing a prophet who told the people to do things the law told them not to. This might seem obvious, that a message opposite to the Scriptures is wrong, but so many people are sucked in by books communicating a heart-wrenching story, a vision of angels, a life-altering experience. Humans cannot rely on their feelings to decide who and what to worship. That's why we have the Word of God. It is the perfect standard.

Mutilators

In Paul's day, people came to the Gentile Christians and told them they had to be circumcised in order to be truly saved. There is nothing wrong with being circumcised. It is not mutilation in itself. Paul circumcised Timothy when he began to be a part of the ministry. Physical things become mutilation when they are works that people say we must have as part of salvation. Justification is by faith alone. A writer whose book demands works as part of salvation is mutilating the faith.

Paul says his former assets are liabilities, because confidence in the flesh is the opposite of confidence in Christ. We cannot save ourselves by our works. People in books can and should do good works, but not as a way to become justified.

Imitators

You might think that an imitator is a fake or a bad thing. But Paul wanted to be an imitator of Christ. During our college years an instructor gave an illustration using a pattern. We lay it on a piece of fabric so that we can cut out something that is exactly the same. But what happens to us, as human beings, when we lay the pattern of Jesus Christ onto our lives and begin cutting? Sometimes God picks us up, holds us side by side with Christ, and says, "You don't look much like My Son."

Some of the people in the books we read, fictional or real, don't look much like Jesus Christ. They are imitating something quite different. We don't want to be influenced by the kinds of books that give us the wrong kinds of patterns to imitate.

Forsake self

Paul, as stated above, tossed everything he once valued -- his human works -- onto the rubbish heap. The pattern of Jewish tradition apart from the Scriptures wasn't making him look much like the Messiah. *It is because of him that I have experienced the loss of all those things. Indeed, I consider them rubbish in order to gain the Messiah.* (v. 8)

Embrace faith

Paul admonished us to do as he had done, to be

> *found in him, not having a righteousness of my own that comes from the Law, but one that comes through the faithfulness of the Messiah, the righteousness that comes from God and*

> *that depends on faith.*
> (Philippians 3:9)

The books we read should teach this need to embrace this change, as Christ has embraced us, wholeheartedly.

Study Christ

> *I want to know the Messiah—what his resurrection power is like and what it means to share in his sufferings by becoming like him in his death, though I hope to experience the resurrection from the dead.* (3:10)

How many books really teach us this kind of passion to know Christ better? How many self-help books really help us toward the goal of being Christlike in every aspect of our lives?

Emulate maturity

> *It's not that I have already reached this goal or have already become perfect. But I keep pursuing it. But this one thing I do: Forgetting what lies behind and straining forward to what lies ahead, I keep pursuing the goal to win the prize of God's heavenly call in the Messiah Jesus.* (3: 12-14)

Read books about the maturing process. Don't dwell on the past, successes or failures, but keep seeking to answer God's call and become more like Christ. Look at it as a prize to be won, not an ordeal to be suffered through.

Anticipate translation

> *Our citizenship, however, is in heaven ... He will change our unassuming bodies and make them like his glorious body* (3: 20-21)

Many books focus on this world, this life, and barely consider heaven. If they do, they focus on near-death experiences with visions of what it will be like, disregarding what it really takes to go there. We get to heaven by *his glorious power*. People practically worship heaven and angels in books, but we must worship Christ and focus on him.

Enemies

The Scriptures take two positions toward enemies. One is praying for their destruction. The other is Jesus Christ's admonition to *love your enemies.* (Matthew 5:24)

Books that manage to balance those perspectives are excellent reading. Paul delivers his warning with a mixture of sadness and finality.

> *For I have often told you, and now tell you even with tears, that many live as enemies of the cross of the Messiah. Their destiny is destruction.* (3: 18-19)

Destiny of destruction

Loving your enemies does not mean you want them to keep on doing evil. Paul reassures believers that these people will not be able to continue to harm believers or the cause of Christ. Their days are numbered.

God of appetite

Easy believism, the prosperity gospel, and any beliefs that allow focus on self fall into the category of making your appetite your god. It is the opposite of everything Paul has been talking about. The shame is that it is common in Christianity.

Glory is shame

We read a blog that decried "divorce parties." The writer was already angry that divorce would be considered a festive occasion. But a reader of his blog iced the cake by sagely justifying multiple divorces. What is wrong becomes right, and is then justified and even celebrated.

Sin and freedom are almost synonymous in many books nowadays. Words are redefined to glorify what should be shameful.

Mind is earthly

For people who truly want to know Christ, the books written by shallow, world-bound people who claim to be Christians are easy to spot. But more and more people are losing their grip on the Scriptures and substituting expert opinions, devotional stories, commentary, studies, and popular sermons for Scriptures.

Chapter Four: Family, Contentment, Generosity

Family

The things you read should treat the godly like family. They should make you long for fellowship with other believers.

Longing to See

Like children who grow up to please their parents, the believers at Philippi were a visible reminder that Paul had been faithful, a glimpse of his victor's crown that Scriptures say believers will receive in heaven. Good reading should keep our eyes fixed on the tasks the Lord would have us accomplish as well as the reward for doing them. It should also encourage us to help other believers to grow, to "stand firm" by allowing them to see the rewards through mature believers.

Urging to Unity

Many have interpreted verse two in the KJV translation *(I beseech Euodias, and beseech Syntyche)* as talking about two women who were so much at odds Paul hesitated to speak their names in the same phrase. Does what you read attempt both to point out and to heal divisions? Both are necessary. Books can point out the need to be a helper to those who seem beyond help because they are so divided; to encourage them by commending their good works of the past; and to keep in mind that even divided workers are important and necessary. Sometimes even nonfiction books focus on divisions because conflict and trouble are more interesting than "smooth sailing." Though normal and untroubled might be "boring," everything possible should be done to restore breaches so that the work can be carried on with all possible strength.

Commending for Work

Do we need reminders that people support us and want us to keep on going, that our names are in the Book of Life, that we are worthy to be called "yokefellows" even with the Apostle Paul? Yes, we do. We sometimes think humility should be groveling but it's important to encourage ourselves by remembering that Christ promises us crowns and other believers are standing behind us cheering us on.

Contentment

Rejoicing

"Keep on rejoicing in the Lord at all times. I will say it again: Keep on rejoicing!" (v. 4) Don't be discouraged. Don't be depressed. Yes, these are human feelings that happen, but Paul wouldn't say this twice if it wasn't possible. Keep away from reading books that depress you, that makes you discontented, that steal your joy. It's not that you should avoid harsh reality. Just make sure it drives you to compassion, selflessness, and prayer for needs, not hopelessness or self-pity. And don't forget that a real danger of books that claim to be uplifting is that readers get a "sugar rush" or energy drink of good feelings that don't last. Beware of empty inspiration that doesn't ground you in the Word of God.

Graciousness

This is related to rejoicing above. Gracious people don't allow themselves to get "down," to be depressed, to "burn out," because they are selfless. They focus on meeting the needs they can, being hospitable, praying, encouraging, forgiving the repentant, and showing grace like God shows it. Many posters and books urge you to cast off "toxic relationships" or shun people who make you feel bad. Sometimes you must do that, but beware of doing it for self-centered reasons. You can't always hang around people who uplift you. Remember, God and your teachers filled you up with the grace they showed you. Go give some of that out, and read books that teach you to do it better.

God's Peace

> *Never worry about anything. Instead, in every situation let your petitions be made known to God through prayers and requests, with thanksgiving. Then God's peace, which goes far beyond anything we can imagine, will guard your hearts and minds in union with the Messiah Jesus.* (vv. 6-7)

Don't read stuff that makes you worry. Financial advice is good if it helps you be generous as well as thrifty. Relationship books are great if they focus you on being spiritually prepared for a mate, for a strong marriage, for a good family dynamic. Anything you read should encourage you to seek God's peace. It should point you toward union with Christ. We need to guard our hearts from worry by prayer in general, by asking for the right things, by being thankful. Our choice of reading material should reinforce those goals.

Praiseworthy

Philippians 4:8-9 break down very simply to practicing, thinking, and doing what meets God's standards for the very best. Paul even encourages them to imitate him. We have got to fill ourselves up with the best of the best when we read so that we will be right ourselves, and be the best possible example.

Generosity

We can express a generous nature even if we have no present means to supply needs. The Philippians either lacked material assets or they couldn't get gifts to Paul right away. Some writers imply that if you are not giving right now just the way they demand that you are heartless. If you are not fixing the world's physical needs as they see them you are selfish. There are ministries that bribe, plead, threaten, and try every means to get you to *give more now*.

Paul did not take this attitude. He still complimented the Philippians because he knew their hearts. They were the only ones who helped in the past and he remembered them fondly for that. He called their gifts pleasing to God, not just pleasing to him.

The flip side of generosity is contentment. Paul got this as a gift from God. Many take Philippians 4:13 out of context and say it means we have unlimited strength to do things. What Paul says here, however, is that we have unlimited strength to not be discontented. *I know how to be humble,* (to live with little fame or money or worldly influence) *and I know how to prosper* (to not go crazy because you have those things). *In each and every situation I have learned the secret of being full and of going hungry, of having too much and of having too little.* Let your reading material teach you contentment. Let it give you God's strength to turn your "wanter" off. Paul does promise that God will supply all their needs. We have to find books that teach us the difference between need and want, though. Glorious riches certainly ought to content us. Christ ought to content us.

Section Two: Avoiding Bad Writing

(from the Book of Numbers)

Chapter One: Beneath the Rules

Why is the Book of Numbers even in the Bible? Many trying to read through the Bible resent its very existence. It's just a bunch of rules and lists. We are not under the law, so can't I ask for grace and just skip it? No you can't, because it contains valuable lessons about bad writing (in the sense of writing that teaches you bad things).

We talked in the Introduction and Part One of this book about the difference between liberty and license. A shocking number of authors either do not understand or deliberately do not teach this difference. It's kind of like the difference between the OT law and the NT grace. People think we get to toss the OT because Jesus died and rose again. Not so. There is way too much talk about Jesus fulfilling the law and none about casting it aside. We can't use the excuse that He was perfect and was the only one who could keep the law. But we can examine what the real purpose of the law is.

More than a Census

The Census in the first part of Numbers was taken for the purpose of organizing society. People first needed to know who was going to protect them, lead them, and intercede for them. So upper and lower age limits and leaders for the military are listed. Many authors today pretend that life is not dangerous and we do not need all this structure and defensive capability. We can unilaterally disarm, pray for peace, hold hands in a circle and sing about tolerance, and everything will be okay. We especially should not make an issue of religion, lest someone be offended. That's a good example of bad writing. We need to listen to God telling us who fights, who leads, and, most important of all, who serves God on our behalf.

Who Fights Wars?

No one under the age of twenty, for starters. Humans have a long history of preferring young warriors, claiming greater stamina, speed, agility, adaptability, but apparently God saw a cutoff in physical, or possibly spiritual, readiness at this age. Studies have been done that indicate the body is not fully mature until around that age, and it makes sense that mentally maturity doesn't normally happen before that age.

Who Leads Clans?

Clan just means broadly extended family. The tribes of Israel, each descended from one of the sons of Jacob, with Joseph represented by Ephraim and Manasseh, were these big families. Exceptions do happen, but the obsession of today's cult of youth evidenced in YA literature is disturbing. The Scriptures say it's a bad thing when children lead. Leadership or advancement in the military is for the experienced and the mature.

There is also a common theme in writing today, that youth is better than maturity. Nowadays when people say mature they mean old. The Scriptures honor maturity. Young people can be mentally mature, but the normal social order should be that elders guide and the young follow and learn to lead as they mature.

Who Serves God?

God has always drawn a line between regular people, all of whom are supposed to be holy and wholeheartedly serving, and the priestly clan of Levi, His set-apart servants to carry out His worship. This is as good a place as any to discuss, again, concepts of freedom and choice, and to add on what personal worthiness means.

Today when people enter full-time service in any religion as a pastor, priest, minister, or whatever the title is, they almost always do so by choice. Modern books are very big on promoting choice or freedom in how, or if, you serve God. People in Numbers did not have a choice. Not about much of anything. The clan of Levi especially did not have a choice about being in the direct, most responsible, and most consequential part of the service of God. Not only did they not get to choose the whether, but they didn't even choose the how. God spelled out exact duties of Aaron's descendants and those of the rest of the subdivisions of Levi.

So these people had no choice about full-time service. Other literature demands that people have to be "called" to serve God. These people were born to serve God. It's not that all the rest of the tribes were off the hook. The point is that all God's people are to serve Him, but in different ways. Service is not a choice. God made us to serve. He also made us to love. These things work in both directions. Adam and Eve were created to love and serve. The infinite God spent to spend personal time with them. Even after they sinned, He was right there. Judging and issuing punishments, yes, because they forced Him to. But He came, and He told them He still loved them, by stating that sin was going to be atoned for. "If that isn't love", as the song says. He even made them their first real clothes.

So God apparently hasn't grasped that "if you love something, set it free" gibberish. He formed us for service and one way or another we will serve. It is our nature. We will serve sin and Satan or God and righteousness. We do not have any other choice. Books that say you have a choice are telling lies. There is no highway between God and Satan where we can coast along, headed in a third direction. It doesn't exist. The insistence of every secularist on the planet cannot create truth out of a lie.

While we are on the subject of priests, there are those writers who admit that people are frail, flawed, and the best kinds of priests and ministers in their books are the ones who have feet of clay and are no longer accepted in the eyes of men to be priests. Those soiled men are the best men, the most compassionate, the best friends. The ones who haven't openly sinned are still useful. They will keep secrets for you. They are under the vow of the confessional, and will never expose your sins.

Before you think you understand any priesthood, or ministry, look at the life of Aaron, Moses' brother. He didn't ask to be Moses' mouthpiece before Pharaoh. He and Moses were joined at the hip for the rest of their lives, because people would always need to hear God's Words, and Aaron would always have to be Moses' spokesman. No choice.

Did Aaron feel fear about this huge burden? Did he experience despair, hopelessness, resentment? We can infer that he did. First came the golden calf incident. The Scriptures don't say much, but some ancient sources say that he was given two choices: Lead the calf worship or be murdered. Perhaps others had already been killed around him. So Aaron caved and made the calf.

Anyone who reads the Old Testament at all is bound to run across people who rebelled and committed acts of idolatry. What did God do to them? Most times they were killed. What happened to Aaron? Nothing that we know of. He went back to being Moses' mouthpiece.

Then came this priesthood thing. Just do it, Aaron. You and your sons. You have no choice. Wash up, put the clothes on, get anointed, sacrifice, sprinkle blood, on and on, the rest of your life. You and your sons, forever. Aaron became High Priest, with his two sons Nadab and Abihu serving under him. A period of purification ensued in which they all had to stay in the tent of meeting. The Scriptures say Aaron's two sons offered strange fire, something the Lord had not commanded, and fire from the Lord killed them. What happened to Aaron? Nothing. We don't even know if he had any responsibility for what happened, but we know that Moses later chastised him because a particular ritual hadn't been carried out correctly. Once again Aaron was forgiven and life went on. Later he and Miriam stirred up trouble over who was the boss. Miriam was struck with leprosy and Aaron was -- well, nothing happened to Aaron, that we know of. Moses struck the rock instead of speaking to it, and Aaron was involved in that, as Moses' spokesman. The only punishment of any kind we know of that he suffered, besides watching what happened to all these people around him, was that he died without going into the Promised Land.

So, when books tell us about these fallen priests, these sinning saints who are more trustworthy because they are no longer so high and mighty perfect, they are telling lies. The priesthood is the most shining example of grace, mercy, and forgiveness by God ever. There are no imperfect people with God, because it's only the blood of Christ that makes men perfect, and it does a complete and stand-alone job of that. It's not a struggle, or a choice, or a lifetime of hard work. God cleansed Aaron and kept cleansing him his whole life. He didn't drown him in the sea or light him on fire or drop him in a crack in the earth or bite him with serpents for his many sins. He forgave. He cleansed. He purified. And He said, "Go on, Aaron. Keep serving me."

Who Camps Where, and Who Travels When

This is just a reinforcement of the specific jobs given to the different groups of people. Protection, leadership, and worship, laid out in physical columns and compass directions, visible to everybody.

Who Demonstrates Obedience?

My favorite part is where it says the people did *exactly what they were told*. How many times are we taught that lesson in other reading material? Don't settle for less. Look for books that reinforce obedience and the observance of God's Word.

Who Rebels Openly?

Nadab and Abihu, as we said before, rebelled openly. The people who demanded the golden calf did also. The list goes on and on. The toll of destruction from disobedience goes on and on. God is a God of love and mercy and forgiveness, as evidenced by Aaron, but people cannot write books to teach unconditional love and forgiving the unrepentant and having no expectation of acceptable service to God. At some point judgment for sin *will* occur.

More Than Just Details

Limitations

Worn out by the endless details of who does what among the sons of Levi? Have you considered that all that "do this, do that" stuff also means you don't have to be overwhelmed by all the needs all around you? Just do *your* job. Don't worry about everyone else's. Many written works try to guilt-trip Christians and say they are ignoring poverty, ignorance, disease, and all the effects of sin, by not working themselves to death fixing man's physical ills. That's what Christians *have* to do. They have to kill themselves with compassion. No, they don't. Scripture lays down limits. To repeat: Do your job. Just your job, with prayer, humility, and faithfulness to God, knowing that it's His job, really, to care for the world.

Age ranges are included in these limits. Books written by the world claim anybody can do anything. Nonsense. Thank God He doesn't expect more of us than He gives us to do. There's a time to begin, and a time to retire, based on physical limitations God graciously gives us.

How dare God exclude people because of physical defects? How can He be so unfair? Today's culture demands laws to make private business owners accommodate handicapped employees. "Reasonable accommodation", though, gets lost in the conflicting cry that people can do whatever they want. People cannot do whatever they want. Limitations are a gracious gift of God. Some of them are temporary. Some of them are permanent. If the Old Testament doesn't make it clear enough for obtuse human brains, *outside the camp* doesn't mean scorned, discarded, "untouchable". It means separated out as a symbol of purification. It doesn't mean impurity, but it requires special, cautious treatment.

Christ didn't say bring all the lepers in and treat them just like the rest of us. He healed some of them and then told them to follow the laws for demonstrating cleansing. We do not have to tolerate spiritual impurity in our churches just to be loving. Christ didn't say come in filthy. He said *go and sin no more*. Numbers talks more about the possibility of purification than it does about "discrimination" against the unclean.

Duties

Just as there are things God does not expect us to do, there are things He does expect us to do. Fundamentally, He expects us to deal with sin. We are not supposed to conceal it. We are not supposed to remain ignorant about it. We are supposed to deal with it. Whatever feminist diatribes hammer into the heads of modern society, the main job of dealing with sin goes to men. Both men and women can commit sin, but men are responsible for dealing with it.

We heard that someone wrote a novel based on the passage in Numbers Five where the wife is suspected of infidelity. In the novel, she is innocent, but the test affects her as if she were guilty. And people also love to ask, why is there no test like this for men? Why, in the

New Testament, was the woman caught in the very act of adultery, but the man is not brought before Jesus, since Old Testament law specified that both were to be punished?

This is secularist thinking. We know throughout history that people were wrongly accused, tried, convicted, and punished in horrible ways or executed for crimes. And the trial by ordeal, where people were subjected to monstrous conditions that wouldn't affect them if they were innocent, is ancient as well. Secularists love to write stories about "false positives" to prove that God is unjust, since these tests were set up by God or His supposed representatives.

We don't have all the answers to why things happen the way they do. We know that no one is innocent before God, because of the sin nature and everyone's personal sin. But we know that *every man did that which was right in his own eyes* tends to lead us into situations like the Benjamites in Judges. Did anybody do anything right in that situation? Yes. They prayed, when things got so bad they didn't know what to do, that God would lead them, and He answered them. There was no happily ever after ending to that story.

Books written by unbelievers definitely advocate that you "follow your heart," exercise your own reason, and toss God's Word out the window. We have no perfect and complete answers for why things go badly in life but we know that laws exist to guide us toward the best outcome. We may not even see that best outcome in this life. Good thing God is in control of eternity, and not man.

The law of the Nazirite here is an example of a completely voluntary vow that can apply to either a man or a woman. We don't know about Samson and why he was conceived under it and required to keep it his entire life. Normally it was temporary and limited. But while you did live under it, you had to be faithful and not do things to break it. God put up with a lot of vow-breaking in Samson's case, since one of the prohibitions was against touching a dead body. Samson made many, many dead bodies, including the lion out of which he ate honey. Samson is another huge example of God's love, mercy, and grace. Instead of being unfair, bullying, and cruel, God delivered His people from the Philistines Samson killed.

The Lord told Moses to teach the priesthood to recite a blessing. Note that no conditions are made about how to get this blessing. Coming on the heels of rituals and laws and involuntary and voluntary activities, it seems that the bottom line is that God wants to bless His people. It is mostly up to us whether we get His blessing, based on our own submission and faithfulness to heed His commandments. We should not expect to perfectly follow or keep the law, but to know the remedies when we sin, and to know that God loves us and wants to bless us.

More than Just Offerings

Sacrifices and offerings are so tedious to read about. At least, the world wants us to think so. Legalistic is a word that's thrown around a lot, even in so-called Christian works. We are to be loving, accepting, tolerant, and so on, and those stinky, bloody, demanding Old Testament law commandments need not apply to us. But why were sacrifices and offerings needed? What were these things for?

Meeting Needs

They were intended to meet needs. First was the need to demonstrate cleansing and purification from sin. But not all offerings were burned up entirely on the altar. Many were brought to the priests and left in their care. Many were partially given to the priests, and partially used for feasts to feed many people and celebrate God's provision. Many were gifts. People gave, and they created abundance by their obedience. The priests had heaps of food and so did the people.

Making Gifts

And not just food. Gold, silver, high-quality wood, textiles -- all kinds of things were given as offerings to the Lord for the building of the tabernacle and at other times, and resulted in obedience and abundance. In spite of what lying history books tell us, the Jewish people were a world power, wealthy, ruling vast areas and receiving tribute (read *offerings to God*), not just ignorant, desert-dwelling sheep herders. Over and over God promises blessing, peace, and great stores of spiritual rewards, not just material things, to those who offer their best to Him.

Creating Abundance

Books that teach you that you don't have to obey God or give to Him rob you of God's abundance. Go ahead and say *my hand has done all these things*. God will let you have your way. But the result will be leanness, not plenty. We know that the consequences of sin include famines, natural disasters, and the suffering, disease, and poverty they bring. Books rail that if God were real, or if He cared, people would have the promised abundance, peace, and safety, so the Bible is a lie. But they deliberately forget that sin is not God's fault. It is man's, and so are the consequences.

More than Just Ceremonies

Requirements

Passover was and is a big ceremony to the Israelites. Symbolically and just on a physical and social level, it is the biggest and most recognizable element of Jewish culture. It was and is a major requirement, to observe Passover. Yet there were people who couldn't celebrate it at the right time because of a death in the family. Not touching a dead body is a recurring commandment, and it happened at Passover time, too, that people died, and other people were present and had to deal with the bodies.

Permissions

So God needed to not only make requirements, He had to extend permissions. Rather than rigidly say, "No, Passover is when it is and you're out of luck if you miss it," God made a "Passover II," if you please, on an alternate date. That's not legalism. That's grace and love. The very fact that there are sacrifices that provide for cleansing shows God's grace and love. People whose books demand freedom from responsibility know nothing of the need to be clean, to be whole, to be restored by God's grace demonstrated by the beauty of the Passover. They can teach us nothing of God's restoration of man through Christ if they can't teach us basic respect for God's laws and ceremonies.

An author friend is writing a fictional account of the Children of Israel in Egypt, the plagues, and the Exodus. She says some people will be offended if she says the Israelites might have been worshiping the false gods of Egypt. They might not have been God's perfect little angels during that time period. Considering the knowledge we have of them after that time, it seems almost certain that some, maybe many, were idolaters.

Christ came to call sinners to repentance. He came as the Great Physician to heal the sick. Don't buy into the lie that the Old Testament God is obsolete. He and Jesus Christ are the same God. They both show love, mercy, and compassion while Christ pleads with us to *Cleanse your hands, you sinners and purify your hearts, you double-minded.* (James 4:8) We are full of *wounds, bruises, and putrefying sores.* (Isaiah 1:6) Lying does not make the problem go away. But Christ our Passover was sacrificed for us. We need to dwell on these thoughts, not the lie that the world teaches, that we can fix ourselves.

More Than Just Scheduling

Going and Staying

The Israelites had their whole lives regimented. When to camp. When to pull up and move. When to sacrifice. When to celebrate. What order to camp in. What order to march in. Sometimes they moved on every day. Sometimes they didn't move for days. God decided when they got water. God decided when they got food. They even had clocks (trumpets) to tell them when to do what.

Is this bondage? Is it legalism? Or is this total provision? Some books warn us against making our lives too stressful by making them too tightly scheduled. Humans can err and harm themselves by having wrong priorities and majoring on minors but God demonstrates here that a disciplined life is an excellent thing. The tabernacle would be set up and taken down according to the direction of the glorious Cloud of God's Presence. The people would set up and break down where and when God told them.

How many people write books and cry out to know God's will for their lives? Here it is: Day by day, be disciplined. Be regimented. Make a schedule. Watch the clock; not to see the hands move toward "quitting time" but to get things done. Stop thinking of "free time" and "me time" and "vacation time". Evans' *Great Doctrines of the Bible* includes an exhortation to consider, instead of planning periodic getaways for pleasure and recreation, planning *prayer vacations*. These were not only times of intensive study, meditation, and prayer, but also of fellowship with believers. The *solemn assemblies* really mean times of getting serious about learning to serve God, not just going around with a long face assuming that following all the rituals will make you holy. *God looks upon the heart.*

Rituals help you remember to get things done. God makes you holy.

Rallying and Rejoicing

Moses invited his brother-in-law from Midian to continue with them. Hobab wasn't sure he wanted to do that. He thought he'd rather go home. Moses urged him to reconsider for two reasons. One, they needed his services as a guide. Wasn't the Shekinah Glory of God leading them good enough? But wait. Moses was really making an offer to Hobab. Serve God's people and you serve God. Be a blessing and God will bless you. You will share in the blessings God gives us if you stick with us and help us. We should not necessarily listen to voices who write that we have to stick close to home, close to family, although those are certainly not sinful in themselves. We have to be willing, sometimes, to strike out away from comfort and familiarity, to help God's people.

Never forget Moses' prayer each time they broke camp or made camp. Here is the promise of God's continued protection and presence. Not the Deist writer's distant, uninvolved God. Not the Master Clockwinder of Theistic Evolution. Certainly not the "God's not there" of the atheist writer's insistence.

> *Whenever the ark was ready to travel, Moses would say: "Arise, LORD, to scatter your enemies, so that whoever hates you will flee from your presence." Whenever the ark was being readied to rest, he would say: "Return, LORD, to the countless thousands of Israel."*
>
> (Numbers 10:35)

Chapter Two: Beneath the Complaints

The Scriptures clearly say that the Israelites experienced real distress. They had to have water. They had to have food. Sometimes these things were genuinely lacking as they traveled. We know this because water did come from rocks. Manna did fall from the sky. Quail did fly in low enough to get clubbed down. Because these things happened, it presupposes that the lack of naturally-occurring resources was very great.

But it is written throughout the wilderness travels that God's glory was visible to them almost daily. They just got reassurances that Hobab was going to guide them to good camping spots. Moses taught them to give and abundance would be given to them. The future was full of promise because of the promises -- the *tangible* reassurances -- of God.

So, by their complaining, they were robbing themselves of a future. They saw provision after provision but refused to remember and persisted in doubting. The Word does not say this series of complaints were because of deprivation. Here begins a cycle of discontent and discipline.

What's to Eat?

Anyone who writes that it's okay to complain to God because He is compassionate and wants to give us everything is playing with fire. And that's what Israel got for their complaints. Fire incinerated some people on the outskirts. Not the core believers. In the next section the Scriptures say that certain people who could not control their appetites actually turned back, headed for the

Egyptian food pots. They had cravings, not needs. Writers who think God is always pleased to grant our "wants" and preach a prosperity gospel err.

> *How we remember the fish that we used to eat in Egypt for free! And the cucumbers, melons, leeks, onions, and garlic!*
>
> (Numbers 11:5)

The worst problem with these complainers was that they sank Moses into a deeply depressed state. He saw no hope of contenting them. He was like a mother with a colicky baby; exhausted by the nonstop crying. Just how long are we supposed to put up with the crying of someone who is not a baby and not sick at all? There are writers who insist that when the Scriptures say *of some have compassion, making a difference,* that we are being told to have infinite patience. Not so.

God's response was to lighten Moses' burden, not immediately to respond to the people's whining one way or the other. Imagine the God of eternity listening to human complaints all these thousands of years. He certainly knew no human being could bear up under it. Seventy elders were chosen to help Moses deal with the people. Moses still didn't quite get it, just as discouragement sometimes blinds and deafens us. He heard God say, "*mumbledy-mumble* *give them meat*" and still thought it was his responsibility. God showed him that it wasn't. The people got meat, but got severe discipline as well, straight from God. A plague struck, and the people learned the price of being unable to control their appetites. God might give us abundance, but we had better ask for self-control, rather than giving in to self-indulgence. Self-help writers often advise Christians to make themselves *comfortable* rather than *in control.*

Who's in Charge?

God had to reassure Moses, to remind him, where the power came from. Some books say it's okay to be discouraged, depressed, or burned out in ministry. But God didn't send Moses on a retreat or to a conference. He gave him help, but he didn't think Moses needed to "come apart before he came apart" as Christian writers like to say. God didn't agree that Moses was burned out and needed to recharge his batteries. Everyone still understood that Moses was the leader, based on Joshua's cry that those two of the seventy who didn't come to the meeting weren't supposed to be prophesying. Moses understood what few books that claim to be inspirational even teach. *I wish all of the LORD's people were prophets and that the LORD would put his spirit upon them!* (Numbers 11:29) God has few leaders he can count on to handle His spiritual gifts. They aren't for everybody. They aren't for people who "open their hearts," or "empty their minds." They are for disciplined, prepared people.

Miriam's name is first for a reason when the Scripture records her rebellion with Aaron. Opinions about the particulars of the wife of Moses mentioned here vary, but God does not fault him for this marriage. He testifies that Moses was humble. Miriam accuses him of being the opposite, of claiming to be God's only spokesperson.

The obvious conclusion was that Miriam was arrogant and sought glory for herself, whereas Moses only sought glory for God through his leadership. God dealt with Miriam for complaining that Moses was getting all the glory. As we said earlier, many despised and ostracized lepers. It was polar opposite to being a leader.

Secularists and other writers have tried to make God a misogynist through this passage. They say God punished a woman for speaking out against male oppression. Miriam's punishment had nothing to do with her being a woman, or being forbidden to speak out. More than one verse calls her a prophetess. She had gifts. God used her among the people to speak His Word. The New Testament Scriptures do, however, say that a woman is not to usurp authority over a man. Miriam didn't get to take Moses' place. Aaron didn't either, for that matter. God's testimony about Moses is worth a careful read. He doesn't say this much about any other man in the Scriptures. Not even close. People idolize Joseph, David, Daniel; but Moses *has been entrusted with my entire household!* says God. (Numbers 12:7, ISV)

Note that Aaron intercedes on Miriam's behalf to Moses. Earlier we mentioned Aaron's lifetime of enforced discipline and the times he seems to have broken out in rebellion. What is worse -- being punished for your sin, or watching someone you love be punished? Aaron is not obviously punished, but he has to endure watching Miriam bear her consequences.

Where Are We Going?

Sending out the spies to explore the land occurs right after this. God says these men were *distinguished leaders*. Their job was to evaluate the land, the people, and the fortifications, and to report back. Some writers teach "a leap of faith," trusting blindly that God will get us to that "milk and honey" place. But true faith is based on tested evidence that what God says is reliable.

How Can We Win?

Moses actually expected the report to encourage these leaders to encourage the people with hard evidence of God's faithfulness. Instead, these trusted leaders lied. The Scriptures call it a *false report*. The majority believed the lie, because, after all, ten trusted leaders said one thing, and only two said another. The majority report is an example of bad literature. It's persuasive speaking to deceive. And it's very commonly imitated, consciously or unconsciously, by writers all over the world, all through time. It represents both a reasonable and an emotional reaction. They concluded that the risks outweighed the benefits.

Who Is to Blame?

Only Joshua and Caleb told the truth. Joshua and Caleb's speech is great literature. What a study in evidence, trust, and obedience. As a reward for one of history's greatest pep talks, also both reasonable and emotional, they were threatened with torture and death. This is how the world reacts to the great message of God's love and provision all the time.

One common theme in modern society is "the blame game." When something goes wrong, people start pointing fingers. Everyone talks about responsibility, but the first impulse is to say, "It wasn't my fault."

So, who was to blame for the report received about the land? Who disheartened the Israelites and drove them to defy God yet again? They blamed Joshua and Caleb, but the responsibility lay with these ten leaders. They abused their influence, and the consequences were disastrous.

Moses interceded for the people when God was ready to destroy them. After the previous few chapters, Moses had amazing grace and love for his people. Or did he? What did he actually say in his prayer? He reminded God that His holiness was at stake. The world would scoff and say, "He couldn't even get those people from Egypt to Canaan. He's just like all the other gods -- unpredictable, short-tempered, violent and murderous." People say that about God anyway, but Moses cared about protecting God's reputation.

Many authors today do not treat God as holy. Many *Christian* authors do not treat Him as holy. They don't defend His reputation before the world. We have heard Christians say they love the "Jesus as surfer dude" image. They want him to "hang out" with everybody, just being a friendly, sweet buddy, especially for sinners.

Jesus did spend time with sinners, but He spent most of his time teaching His disciples about God's love, provision, and holiness.

Chapter Three: Beneath the Rebellions

Many books portray rebellions against oppressive rulers. Rebellion is a good thing. After all, look how it turned out for America. So even Christians confidently preach that because "we are not under the law, we are under grace," that the Old Testament Law only has value as object lessons of oppression, misogyny, cruelty, and across the board unfairness. The Old Testament God was divisive, terrifying, and we are so glad we don't have to listen to that anymore.

Of course, people do not so obviously undermine the authority of the Scriptures and create a "pick what you want" buffet of belief. Usually it is much more subtle. The message, however, is clear to anyone with wit to understand. Ignore most of the Old Testament, particularly the Law, because that was the old, harsh, judgmental, unfair God. We have a shiny, sweet, new god for you. He's always loving, kind, fair, generous, and you'll be comfortable and happy forever.

Rules Kept and Broken

So it is good that here in the dreaded book of Numbers, God gives us clear examples of things that are voluntary, celebratory, inclusive, and designed to comfort and encourage believers of all kinds.

Festivals

Requirements for sacrifices and offerings are always quite specific. This is part of the discipline God is trying to teach people. All the way back to Cain and the first sacrifice, we have learned that you can't just approach God any old way. This is not because God is picky and unreasonable, but because things have to be done a certain way. Why can't we trust that the Creator of the universe knows how things are supposed to work? God's chosen people, the Children of Israel, all had to do things just right, and just the same way. But here's the good part.

> *Now, if a resident alien lives with you, or whoever else is with you throughout your generations, let him make an offering made by fire, a pleasing aroma to the LORD. Just as you do, so is he to do.* (Numbers 15:14)

A resident alien is a foreign-born person who wants to live among the Israelites. He also wants to worship the true God. Now, in different places, God makes demands on resident aliens distinct from Israelites native-born. But here the requirements are exactly the same. God is not a xenophobe. He does not hate other races or any kind of foreigner. He loves everyone, and He extends the same privilege of worship to everyone equally.

So when anybody tells you God hates blacks, or anybody who is different, bring them to this book and point them to this verse. Same rules for everybody. Everybody is free to come to God. Everybody has rules to follow, but they are exactly the same rules. Give God the first, give God the best, give God what He asks for.

The other important point here is that God does forgive. He forgives everybody, not just the Israelites. He forgives in the same way, by the same rules, even when you screw up and don't realize you've screwed up. *Inadvertent sins* are accidents. God does allow for them. They are still sins, and they still need atonement. But God generously makes provision. He's not mean, restrictive, and out to punish. He's out to love, give guidance, and forgive.

Sabbath-breaking

Don't forget that those who despise God's commands are treated equally too. That's why the man gathering wood on the Sabbath was stoned. Oh, how unfair; oh, how cruel. No. Right before that verses warn about defiance, acting *with a high hand,* blaspheming. A clear distinction is made between those who choose to follow God, but make mistakes, and those who act defiantly.

The Blue Border

This is actually sometimes translated blue or purple, based on a dye used in ancient times, but the color isn't as important as the point about separation. God said this border of cord with tassels was a reminder. Look at the border, remember the commandments, stay away from the sins. Separate yourself from self-centeredness. Notice it doesn't say a word about those naughty heathens they weren't supposed to imitate when they came into the land. It warns against *your own interests and desires that lead you to be unfaithful.* (Numbers 15:39)

Some writers teach that *Come out from among them and be ye separate* means that if you just get away from bad people you will be good. Another secularist lie teaches that everyone has some good inside him somewhere. See how confusing things get when man tries to teach from his own confused reasoning?

But there is another old saying that wherever you may run, you can't get away from yourself. As the Scriptures say, it isn't what goes into you that defiles you, it's what comes out. From the heart comes all manner of wickedness.

Leadership Defied and Honored

Korah

Korah, Dathan, and Abiram clearly did not get the memo about the lesson Miriam and Aaron learned. Once again we have well-known men who were *representatives* from the assembly, similar to the ten spies. Many famous and respected authors have enormous influence, just like these men did. Yet they stand up with people who ought to know better and support a rebellion.

The phrase they use to attack Moses is very significant. They said, *You have appropriated too much for yourselves from the entire congregation.* They accused Moses of enriching himself at the people's expense. So they went beyond Miriam's accusation of pride in his leadership and accused him of corruption. Just for good measure they threw in that self-righteous *all the people are holy* line. Possibly they wanted a "piece of the action." The way they put it was that they considered themselves just as deserving of "reward for service" as Moses. But it was a false charge.

How does this apply to bad writing? People frequently accuse God's servants of being "in it for the money." Sometimes this turns out to be the case. Most people can name so-called servants of God who turned out to be taking offerings and turning them into lavish lifestyles. But others simply accuse all believers of trying to scam people when they ask for monetary support. We have all become suspicious of every ministry, every fundraiser, every request for donations, and God's works suffers because writers echo the cry of these men that leaders in God's work are trying to rob people. Those missionaries and ministries just need to have faith a God will provide, right? Why don't they stop begging for money and pray to God?

Censers

The censer test shows that God does not discriminate. Everyone had an equal chance to offer incense to the Lord. Each man provided his own censer, so it was in no way "rigged." Each one who rebelled was incinerated. Those who refused to come were swallowed up, along with everything and everybody connected with them. Secularists cry that this is unfair, since wives and children were also killed. Notice the announcement

Moses made. Everyone who was not connected to them had to pull up stakes and move away. Nothing in the Scriptures say that there was a prohibition against Korah, Dathan, and Abiram's families moving away as well. Nobody had to die. This was unbelief on an unbelievable scale. They simply defied the authority of Moses and of God. The next day people still complained that Moses and Aaron were to blame for these deaths, and God made it clear to them again. Aaron saved untold lives that day by using his censer to stop a plague that killed almost 15,000 more. This was death because of defiance and disobedience based on unbelief. People today put that defiance into print all the time.

Rods

One last test was supposed to convince the Israelites. Aaron's rod budded and produced almonds, demonstrating his family alone was to fill the offices of the priesthood. The rod was to remain as a visible sign of God's command, to stop the complaints, *so that they won't die*. Yet the people went out of the tent and said, *We're all going to die!* It's good to fear God and reverence His power, but this smacks of continued unbelief. Writers reject the God of the Bible as too scary. They turn away from that beautiful harvest of ripe almonds that once again showed His love for the obedient and provision for selfless servants.

Unbelief still ruled in many hearts, and it still does today, when writers do not treat God as holy, and His Word as authoritative. He gives commands so that people don't die, evidence that His authority is reliable, and writers turn right around and offer that buffet of "whatever you want to believe" Christianity.

Purification Needed and Observed

The Gift of the Priesthood

I played devil's advocate earlier by saying that some writers treat service like the Aaronic priesthood as a type of determinism. Aaron and his descendants had no choice. But in Numbers Eighteen God says, *I'm giving you the priesthood as a gift of service.* He also admonishes Aaron that he should invite his relatives, that they are His gift for the ministry, but that only authorized people may fill the holy offices.

Note that this blessing includes all people, in terms of the provision of the priesthood being God's gracious gift to us as well. Though we don't live under the Levitical system today, we all need to be taught holiness and have that example living before us. People who write books about teachers of the Word being judgmental, repressive, and legalistic do not understand what a gift it is to have someone show us an example of purity and separation from sin to help equip us for service to God.

So, far from being enslavement, the priesthood is a gift to Aaron and his descendants. His family, the rest of the tribe of Levi, were a gift to him to assist. This was to be God's gracious provision for the tribe of Levi. They had no physical inheritance in the land, but the people had the blessing of providing for them. Remember the earlier promises of abundant provision for abundant giving? Gifts from God all around.

How many people try to determine God's will for their lives? Some write books about it and struggle all their lives with the question. Aaron and the Levites didn't have to. Isn't it true, though, that many people who claim they are searching for God's will or who claim not to know it, and write books about their search, are actually guilty of one of two sins? One, they do not earnestly study the Word of God, but study man's opinion in other books or human council. It's hard to know what someone wants you to do if you pay attention to everyone but Him. Two, they have found it out but they don't want to do it.

The Need for the Red Heifer

Calling someone unclean is considered by the world today to be discrimination. It's true that in the New Testament God prepared Peter to minister to Cornelius and his household by the vision of the mixture of living things in the sheet. It was the custom of Jews to separate themselves from Gentiles, but that needed to change if the Jews were going to communicate Christ to the Gentiles.

However, back here in the Old Testament, at least, the unclean could do things others could not. Part of the ritual of the Red Heifer, and many other sacrifices, included carrying out ashes. Either someone had to make himself unclean to do that, or someone who was already unclean could. Everything isn't always fair or equal. No one gets treated as perfectly as he or she might wish. But everyone has a God-given purpose, even if, right now, it's being unclean so you can carry out the ashes. That was still service to God.

Note that there were remedies for ceremonial uncleanness. God didn't leave people twisting in the wind, ostracized from society, forever. He gave specific steps to follow, time to elapse, and then the unclean was clean again in almost all cases except serious, contagious illness. This, too, is a lesson to us, since not everything can be solved by banning discrimination. If a person is ill and his disease can be transmitted to others, it is not discrimination to take reasonable health precautions to protect others from catching his illness.

When secularist (or shallow Christian writers who try to emulate them) take up this subject, they cry discrimination. Disease, decomposition, and contaminants don't phase them. The Bible should be ignored because parts of it teach that some things and people are unclean. That is so unloving, superstitious, and just plain mean. Naturally the physical is a picture of the spiritual here, as in many places in the Bible, and the unbelievers will take any chance to turn people against reading the Scriptures. They do not want people to learn how to become spiritually clean.

Obedience Demanded and Enforced

Moses' sin

After all Moses went through, defending the people against God's wrath, carrying them along through all this time and trouble, modern writers would say he deserved some slack here. The New Testament says we have to forgive seventy times seven, so why did God come down so hard on Moses? It's just not fair.

But God calls Moses' sin unbelief. Over and over, Moses demonstrated belief in his face-to-face relationship with God, in the trials and tribulations of leading those people. This time, what he did expressed unbelief. People who write books that teach easy-believism, that God will take you however and wherever you are, all that matters is that you love Jesus -- look at Moses.

Look hard. Try to understand that over and over Moses defended and argued for God's holiness, God's absolute standard of obedience as an expression of belief. But here, he threw the Promised Land away by a couple of whacks with a stick. God didn't deprive him of it. He chose to do the wrong thing, publicly. Note that in later chapters Moses does point out that the people bear a part of the responsibility, saying God did it *for your sakes*. We all make our own decisions, to sin or not to sin, but Many writers harp so long and loud about our "needs," our rights, our freedoms, about how people have to be accepting, to show tolerance and unconditional love, they can wear down the resistance of a man who stood for God all his life and tempt him to sin. Don't be that writer.

Aaron's death

Only Moses and Eleazar attended Aaron's death. The last memory Aaron had on this earth was Moses removing his priestly garments to put them on Eleazar. And what a memory that must have been for Eleazar. Did he know all that his father had done in his life? Most likely this was a time of deep reflection for Eleazar. Earthly writers would have urged us to "remember only the good things," but God reminded Eleazar one more time of the failure of his father, Israel's high priest, to treat God as holy. We as writers have got to take the opportunities God gives us to remind people: nothing is more important than God's holiness. Later on we will see the impression that made on Eleazar.

Chapter Four: Beneath the Nations' Refusals

It was almost time for Israel to enter the land, chronologically. They were getting close to the nations surrounding their Promised Land, and it was time to exercise some diplomacy. Secular writers will say we always have to use diplomacy, to seek peace instead of war, to make every possible concession to avoid conflict. But God's commands were simple and straightforward.

Edom

Remember that the people of Edom were the descendants of Esau, the brother of Jacob. They were cousins to the Israelites. But there was little love or trust between them. God made it clear that Israel: 1. wasn't planning to take Edom's land; 2. Didn't need anything from them that they couldn't pay for; 3. Wouldn't trespass or take a thing; just stay on the highway.

God says, *"Jacob have I loved, and Esau have I hated."* (Romans 9:13, based on Malachi 1) There is even an award-winning novel that uses part of this verse in its title. Secularists again cry that God is unfair, to love one group of people and hate another. But the history of Edom is to disobey God, to despise His provision, to "do his own thing," all the way back to Esau himself. Here it is again -- the reason why Edom has earned God's displeasure, generation after generation. The people react in rage and swear there will be war if Israel doesn't detour around Edom.

There are two lessons for writers here: One is that people earn God's wrath. He doesn't just throw it out for no reason. Two is that even if people have earned wrath, there is room for repentance. Edom did what the world does and teaches. It looked out for Number One. It reinforced its national defiance against God. The people clearly understood the conditions and they still had no trust in God or in their relatives. There was no compassion, no tolerance, no taking advantage of a chance to reconcile. Who is truly being "unfair?"

Impatience

Canaanites actually had choices. Everyone thinks, because ungodly writers love to repeat it, that they were always and forever devoted to destruction and that God had it in for them. They were hopeless and helpless, bullied into extinction by that mean old God. Hundreds of years ago God said *their iniquity is not yet full.* What He meant was that anywhere along the way, people can repent. They don't have to keep filling the sin container. God had specific commands for foreigners to be accepted into the Israelite community, like Rahab and her family were.

People could also leave, and some did. There is evidence that tribes like the Yoruba in Africa may be descended from middle-eastern migrants. Some archaeologists think many Canaanites may have left the land in safety and resettled elsewhere. Over and over in the conquest of the land the story is the same. The people would not repent. They would not turn to God. They just kept attacking. And they sealed their own fates.

So, these Canaanites attacked and God gave victory over them through prayer. But the Israelites still had to go a roundabout way to arrive where God told them. With a victory already under their belts, they still couldn't be patient. Perhaps the attacking Canaanites made them nervous. Whatever the reason, all the old, ugly complaining started again.

Serpents

People often write that they don't need to read or study the Bible because they already know all about God. It is astonishing that they can be so knowledgeable, because the one thing that stands out about God, all the way through the Bible, is how He acts so differently in situations. This time God sent poisonous serpents to bite the people who complained.

He also provided an unusual remedy when they prayed for help. *Look and live* at a bronze serpent on a pole. Jesus Christ brought this up as foreshadowing of His own death and atonement. Only shallow people think they know everything there is to know about God. Or is it that they just want to discourage you from learning about Him by complaining that He is boring and so is His Word?

God even provided water by a different method this time. It says all the rulers sang and dug a well for the people. God is certainly not boring or predictable. So it must be that those who write to say He is are liars.

Amorites, Ammon, Bashan

Sihon, king of the Amorites, had a chance here. God gave him the same proposal He made to Edom. The difference was that Sihon didn't just threaten war; he came out with an army. There is no unfairness here. God did not bully Sihon, or the Ammonites, or Bashan. They came out in unilateral aggression. Should Israel have sat in a circle singing about peace while these nations attacked? Of course not.

Moabites and Midianites

Abusing God's Power

We don't know exactly who or what Balaam was, except that God spoke to him, and people considered him a powerful and reliable person. Balaam got results. This person who is so puzzling to true believers is actually a common character in worldly writing. Few people haven't read about a renowned magician whose power comes from an unknown source.

We find it interesting that the God Who gave Balaam his power seems to have been unknown to Balak. He knew this God to be powerful, reliable, and Balaam to be His spokesperson. Why did Balaam not tell people who this God was? Would he have diminished his power and reputation? Many writers make a mystery out of God and His Word, even while claiming to be believers. They say it's too difficult for ordinary people to understand. We end up with more op-ed writers than we do plain teachers of the Word.

People did not know how Balaam got to be powerful, but he capitalized on that reputation, in the most literal sense. We know he had real power and made real money because Balak promised him great riches to do that little cursing job. *Whomever you bless is blessed and whomever you curse is cursed.* (Numbers 22:6) Did God only allow Balaam to use His power against people who needed cursing before this? We don't know, but clearly Balaam understood his limits, and actually said no to the first delegation. Interesting that the delegation did not report what Balaam actually said to Balaak. They either didn't understand or didn't care that there was a God behind Balaam's ability to perform. The magician was being temperamental, refusing to perform. He must want more money.

How often the world looks for a magic charm to solve its problems. All kinds of books are written about how to tap into spiritual power. Some are based on a specific religion, but a growing number rely on harnessing some sort of power without talking about its real source. The writers might call it natural or cosmic or some other sort of energy, and you are not really supposed to inquire where it comes from. Scary, isn't it? Scary that people don't really care about the source of power. They may even call it God, but they just want it to do stuff. They don't want to study the Scriptures or accept God's authority. They just want the magic charms, and they can pay for them, so please leave that silly responsibility stuff out of the picture.

Protecting God's People

Don't go with them. Don't curse the people, because they're blessed.

This is a critical standard for writing. Secularist writers will seek any and all methods of undermining and destroying God's Word and His people. Balaam looked for any way he could to collect Balak's money, and eventually suggested a way to get the Israelites to corrupt themselves. Secularists have subtly and not-so-subtly infiltrated Christianity with all kinds of loose standards based on fairness, tolerance, diversity, multiculturalism, and just plain old abandonment of discipline, purity of person, and doctrine. The result is hopeless and helpless churches.

Balak did not get the message, by the way. He kept trying to figure out a way to destroy God's people. The persistence in the secularist attacks in published works is just as strong. They will not be talked out of doing harm to believers. Their thinking and understanding becomes so narrow as they continually plan assaults that it almost becomes laughable. But we should not be like writers who laugh at the ungodly and toss off phrases like "God's got this" and "If the devil doesn't like it he can sit on a tack." The Scriptures say that we can laugh at the ungodly when we see God's wrath chasing them over the horizon, and not before.

Corrupting God's Leaders

We are told in other Scriptures that what happened at Shittim, the site of Israel's sin in joining with the Baal-peor cult, was a result of Balaam's counsel to Balak. Balaam was a believer in the most high God. That is clear, since he is repeatedly described as hearing God speak and communicating his message.

We do not understand how someone like that could fall into that sin, but God's servants can be corrupted by greed. Books are being written today by professing Christians that teach prosperity, success, and other kinds of personal, earthly enrichment, and offer little or no true spiritual food. And they advocate ungodly practices to achieve success or wealth.

We read a newspaper article and saw photos years ago about a stripper invited to perform in a church. It was not satirical or intended as comedy or mockery. We can't even imagine what the real purpose was, but it is an example of what we should not use as a ministry tool. Someone apparently did, however.

Yoga and other forms of eastern exercise are frequently offered in churches. We just read an article stating the author's opinion that Yoga, Tai chi, and Qigong are all potential doorways into the occult. People howl in disbelief if you tell them this. If you are told to do something that "opens your mind," "expands your consciousness," or involves "focused intentions," please beware. Aleister Crowley, black magic practitioner and Satanist church founder, said that special body positioning, willpower, and focused intentions are tools he used for his witchcraft.

Sex has enormous influence on the thinking of all people, saved and unsaved. Christians have been blamed for centuries for warping people's thinking as well as accused of horrible sexual crimes. Secularists want us to believe that this is the norm; that there are no Christians with healthy sexual appetites and expressions. Their idea of healthy is hedonistic, of course. The only true attitude is to allow everything and anything.

Churches are being pressured, and many have already caved in, to accept practicing homosexuals as full members and to ordain them and also women as ministers. This is a necessary conditioning to get believers to toss out the authority of the Scriptures. That's the entire purpose of the breaking down of sexual barriers. Don't believe the Bible. You're interpreting it wrong. You're translating it wrong. Whatever argument works, you must give up cherished truth or you are not being loving and accepting. You will never reach the lost if you preach against sexual equality and freedom. They won't come to church and sit with a bunch of prudes. They won't be judged. They won't accept that anything outside of repentance, purity, and traditional marriage is wrong.

These arguments have not changed in thousands of years. They worked with the Israelites. Why else would *Salu's son Zimri, a leader from the tribe of Simeon* (Numbers 25:14) bring that Midianite princess Cozbi right into the camp and have sex with her? It wasn't enough for them to go worship at the cult center. It had to infiltrate into the highest ranks of Israel and walk openly into the camp, or the indoctrination failed.

What is the answer when sexual license comes into your church and someone demands that you not only accept it but welcome it and put it on public display? Here is the evidence of what Eleazar learned from watching his father Aaron die outside the land after failing to defend God's holiness. Here's the lesson he communicated to his son Phinehas. Flaunt sexual sin in my face? Pull it in among my people, in front of my church? Start death burning through my friends, my family, and my God's holy place? Here I come, spear in hand. Don't take an opportunity to practice your unconditional love for that man and embrace his filthy, idolatrous, x-rated performance. Deal with it. Stop the plague. Save the people who haven't yet been contaminated.

This also resulted in God's command to execute the Midianites. Midianites, Ammonites, and Moabites were relatives of the Israelites through Abraham. God did not originally include them among the nations to purge out of the land. But they came under God's judgment for attacking Israel and for corrupting practices. They brought it on themselves. It was not unfair.

Chapter Five: Beneath the New Census

Does it seem like we're starting over again? This is everything you said you hated about Numbers in the first place. Another census. Another long list of unpronounceable names. Nobody in their right mind expects people to read this stuff. This is the undisciplined mindset of writers today. They want to tickle your ears with stuff that's interesting to you, when God expects us to build up our attention spans so we can listen long and hard to what He needs us to know.

Purging Rebellion

The new census shows a new crop of Israelites. Israel's second chance, or new hope for the promised land. We have seen people killed by plagues, by fire, by being swallowed up by the earth, and a hundred or more people died every day for one reason or another.

Providing Equality

No census in the Bible ever mentions women, of course. Secularists and feminists insist that women don't count in the Bible. They're just oppressed and dominated. Lot's wife, and so many others, aren't even named.

The truth is that here in Numbers 27, a group of women is named, and their story is a critical point to refute secularist writings that undermine the authority of the Scriptures. Mahlah, Noah, Hoglah, Milcah, and Tirzah are daughters of Zelophehad, a man who had no sons. They were free to approach Moses and Israel's judges just like men could. They made a request that most secularists would deny was even in the Bible. "Give us property in the Promised Land just like sons get." And the answer from God Himself? *You are certainly to give to them a possession for an inheritance among their father's relatives.* Daughters inherited before other male relatives, such as uncles or cousins, if there were no sons in the immediate family. Most secularists will tell you stories of women excluded from the family property, usurped by unscrupulous male relatives, kicked out with nothing. Stories like that aren't in the Bible.

Securing Succession

There was a condition for women inheriting their fathers' property, though. It was also done in the name of fairness. Certain lands belonged to certain tribes. That ownership within that tribe was non-negotiable. So these women had to agree that they would only marry men within their own tribe. Land given by God to the tribe of Judah,for example, could not be taken over by Simeon's tribe. A daughter of Judah who inherited her father's land could not marry a man from Simeon. Though it is not openly stated here, the Scriptures imply that this means women had a choice about who to marry. Secularists love to claim that in the Bible arranged marriages were the only possibility and women were transferred like chattel. They need to tell the truth.

Sanctifying Obedience

Here are very exacting requirements for sacrifices in the matters of timing, type, and regularity. Sacrifices are also tied to festivals. Those also have very specific requirements. The good thing is that God gives all these specifics very clearly so there's no excuse for not knowing. People wring their hands and cry, "What's God's Will for my life?" or write book after book claiming to tell people that "Do what you dream," "Listen to your heart," and "Trust your feelings" are messages from God.

God speaks through His Word. It's already written down. *It's clear, literal, and simply takes devotion and discipline to understand.* People want to throw out everything in the Bible that takes any patience or persistence to figure out. Learn the meaning of unleavened bread. Find out why sometimes a lamb was the right sacrifice and sometimes a bull was necessary. Understanding what God wants from us is not impossible. It's not easy, but it can be done with faithful study of His Word.

Note in many places that sacrifices and offerings are amended in cases of financial hardship. Pigeons are good if you can't afford lambs, for example. God is gracious, not unreasonable. He planned for the people to have abundance but He knew sin spilled over and made people poor.

Voluntary Vows

People were allowed to make promises in a public, binding way, but it was not a requirement. If they did, they had to keep that vow, no matter what. The one exception was a woman, because her father (if unmarried) or her husband could say, "No, you can't make that vow."

This doesn't mean a woman was oppressed by men and unable to make her own decisions. These men had the option of saying nothing and letting the vow stand. It was simply a safety valve against women making rash decisions. It was protection, not oppression.

Chapter Six: Beneath the Conquest and Division

The last part of Numbers deals with the beginning stages of the conquest of the land. Consider all the songs and writings devoted to applying Israel's issues to believers and you'll understand that this is not at all irrelevant reading. In fact, a case might be made against bad writing that regurgitates Scriptural principles but doesn't make a correct application, or replaces real understanding and teaching with patched-on applications.

Transfer of Moses' Authority

In Numbers 27, Moses is told he will soon die. Moses' response is stellar. He asks God to appoint his replacement. He thinks of God's people first and wants them to have a good leader. How many writers have built an empire on themselves but have made no provision for the future care of the ministry they established. Too many ministries crumble when the founder dies. God's people went on because Joshua was a man prepared by God for years before the ceremony officially making him leader. Today's secularist culture creates worship of individuals. People idolize actors and even politicians and scientists. That's why politicians can get re-elected their whole lives, and why it's called "pop-science."

Admonition to Future Obedience

You cannot say that the people were not fully responsible for obeying the Lord's commands through Recently a plane crashed on takeoff. No lives were lost except three passengers who did not have their seatbelts fastened. On every flight, an attendant goes through the procedures and an announcement comes over the PA to fasten seatbelts, complete with instructions on how to do it. It's boring. People who have flown more than twice know it by heart. But to ignore it just because it's repetition is to court death.

Don't think God's commands are as important as fastening your seatbelt on takeoff? How can you skip over what the Creator of the Universe considers important enough to repeat? Secularists want to titillate you with what's new and different. Many writers want you to ignore old, boring, out-of-date legalism. All of these voices cry that the Scriptures are not authoritative on the basis that they are ... boring. Really? That's the argument? Please ignore them and take the time to know God's Word as thoroughly as you can.

Warning of Penalty for Failure

> *Look! These women were the same ones who were counseled by Balaam to cause the Israelis to commit a grievous sin against the LORD at Peor. As a result, that plague infected the LORD's community.*
> (Numbers 31: 16)

Here we learn two things: One, exactly how Balaam finally earned Balak's money. Two, we learn that people were still making up ways to serve God and ignoring crystal-clear commands. Destroy all means *destroy all.* Women who had helped seduce the Israelites were brought along as spoil, and that was against God's command. The soldiers risked more death by this disobedience, as Moses reminds them. Moses also reminded them of the need for purification of everything, living and non-living. Yes, it was hard to kill women and children. Yes, it went against their human feelings. Almost everything we have ever read outside the Bible admonishes us to rescue and defend women and children. But God knows better than we do about these things. Like other places in the Law of Moses, where a tiny contamination in a house could spread into a deadly infestation, even one woman or one child could cause Israel to sin again. We have to trust God more than our sin-blinded instincts and feelings.

Provision for Priesthood

One of the ways in which God provided for the priesthood and the whole tribe of Levi was through taxing spoils of war. We don't like taxes most of the time. But this was a good tax. It helped to make sure God's most direct servants were provided for. In Nehemiah 13, corruption settles in again soon after the remnant returns to the land. Nehemiah returns from Babylon to find that the Levites have not been given their tithes and tax revenues and they have been forced to leave God's service and seek to feed themselves by tending the fields.

Secularists like to mock the concept of God's workers being supported by God's people. They ask why God doesn't directly and miraculously give people what they need. Even believers claim there is an endless barrage of requests for funding from every missionary, every ministry, and that they just give up trying to decide what to give to and light-heartedly say "God will take care of them," or "I'll pray for them." We all have our own financial demands, and some really are struggling.

But God has given us the gift of supporting His workers. We have got to understand that this is a gift, not a burden, and we need to take it seriously. After all, it comes from One who has infinite ability to provide for these needs Himself, but chooses to let us do it. And remember, earlier in Numbers, that God promised abundant provision would follow abundant giving.

> *Bring ye all the tithes into the storehouse, that there may be meat in mine house, and prove me now herewith, saith the LORD of hosts, if I will not open you the windows of heaven, and*

> *pour you out a blessing, that there shall not be room enough to receive it.* (Malachi 3:10)

People have suffered privations because they refused to be generous. This is the truth, whatever people want you to believe. "You have to look after Number One" is not a biblical principle.

Blood Pollutes the Land

> *You are not to pollute the land where you live, because blood defiles the land, and the land cannot atone for blood that has been spilled on it, except through the blood of the one who spilled it. You are not to defile the land where you will be living, because I'm living among you. I am the LORD, who lives in Israel.* (Numbers 35:28)

So many people, secularists and Christians, are against the death penalty that it's scary. So many are pro-choice (encourage, not just allow, killing unborn babies). So many, even when they do acknowledge an act of violence as a crime, give slap-on-the-wrist penalties for polluting the world with blood.

Violence is so common. So much is ignored. And the legal attacks come against home defenders and those who carry weapons to protect themselves. It is as if those who are supposed to protect the land from being polluted crave more pollution. Writers defend violence by condemning every kind of preventative.

Pro-life speakers are jailed to shut their mouths. Murders become folk-heroes because of their value as campaign issues. Bloodshed stains the world and secularists continue to cry out for tolerance, forgiveness, and disarming on the part of the victims. It's as if they serve a god that demands hourly blood sacrifices and have to appease him. Oh, wait ... they do.

I John 3, among other passages, says that Satan is a liar. He wants to turn God's commands inside out and pervert our minds to believe the opposite of what God teaches us. In ancient myths the "Trickster" god is the good guy. He helps man when the father god or creator beats them down and oppresses them. Satan told Eve eating the fruit was good. He's been telling us evil is good ever since, and his minions repeat the same message over and over from the distant past to today. Don't listen to him or them. Listen to God.

Section Three: Ugly or Pretty, These Are Must-Have Standards (from the Book of Proverbs)

Two Choices: Fear God or Be a Fool

The fear of the LORD is the beginning of knowledge. (Ch 1:7a)

Fear is a catchword that riles up the secularist writers. They teach us not to fear anything. All kinds of terminology has been invented to make humans believe they 1. are under no authority, 2. have no responsibility, and 3. bear no consequences for their actions. So there is nothing to fear.

Of course people have not entirely succumbed to that thinking, and still display some sense. But more and more we see the consequences of teaching people to be fearless. On the surface it seems like a good thing, not to be afraid. But the Scriptures make it clear, over and over, in practically every chapter of every book, that we must fear God.

Defining the Fear of God

He Can Eternally Condemn Us

Listen to the words of Jesus Christ. People were stepping on each other to listen to His words, but he addressed His disciples first of all.

> *And I say unto you my friends, Be not afraid of them that kill the body, and after that have no more that they can do. But I will forewarn you whom ye shall fear: Fear him, which after he hath killed hath power to cast into hell; yea, I say unto you, Fear him.*
> (Luke 12:4)

Who is He talking about? Even secularists will be waving their hands in the air to answer that one. "Oooh! Oooh! I know! Pick me! It's *God!*"

He Can Expose our Hypocrisy

And they are right. The passage in Luke 12 begins with Jesus telling the disciples not to let the Pharisees corrupt them with hypocrisy. Hypocrisy is when you say one thing and do another, of course. It's when you hide your evil nature by pretending to be a goody-two-shoes. Everybody hates a hypocrite. Christ says what you are, what you've tried to hide, will be exposed. By who? By *God,* of course.

The Pharisees, Sadducees, and Jewish leaders had lots of power. Through the Roman government they even managed to kill Jesus Christ. That's what it means by killing the body. But Christ said not to fear human beings, who can only kill your body. In the Garden of Gethsemane He didn't sweat blood because the Jewish officials were coming to get Him. He sweat blood because he was all alone before the God of glory wrestling for the eternal souls of every member of His blind, stupid, sinful pinnacle of Creation: Man. He was afraid of the God Who had said to Moses,

> *Now therefore let me alone, that my wrath may wax hot against them, and that I may consume them: and I will make of thee a great nation.* (Exodus 32:10)

Many people who write self-help books genuinely want to teach people something. The grand idea behind such books is to help people learn to be better in some way. Still, most aspiring authors also have in the back of their minds the idea that they might get rich as the author of a bestseller. Once a book actually becomes successful, the author tries to repeat that success. In public he will probably say he still just wants to help people.

But the content of many of these self-help books is so vaguely inspirational and recycled from what others have already written, rather than concretely helpful, that you have to wonder what was foremost in the author's mind.

Another kind of inspirational author is the "feel good" kind. He doesn't point out sin. He doesn't *refute, warn, and encourage with the utmost patience when you teach.* (2 Timothy 4:4) He might make you cry, but they will be tears of joy because you will be so happy that he demands nothing from you. He expects no change. This kind of writing can do a great deal of harm because people are encouraged to think of themselves as Christians when they don't even believe they have any sins to repent of. This "tolerant-of-everything" writer is much like what Dorothy L. Sayer condemned:

> "In the world it is called Tolerance, but in hell it is called Despair...the sin that believes in nothing, cares for nothing, seeks to know nothing, interferes with nothing, enjoys nothing, hates nothing, finds purpose in nothing, lives for nothing, and remains alive because there is nothing for which it will die."

He Can Defeat Our Ambitions

We mentioned before that people hate hypocrites. Sometimes an author is claiming to serve God when he's really only trying to increase his wealth. *No one can serve two masters, because either he will hate one and love the other, or be loyal to one and despise the other. You cannot serve God and riches!* (Matthew 6:24, ISV)

So-called believers try to water this word "fear" down and call it respect or reverence, not fear. We had better show those toward God, certainly, but the word *fear* simply occurs too many times to allow for redefining it. God is the One Who can cast body and soul into hell. Jesus Christ, God the Son, come in the flesh, feared His own Father, for the sake of His beloved Creation. Why in the world wouldn't we?

Secularist writers redefine words to rob them of their real power and give them different powers. To them the word fear should not exist, because it is so inextricably intertwined with bowing down to powers greater than themselves. They redefine authority as oppression. Responsibility becomes imprisonment. Consequences become unfairness. If you buy into the secularist line you will spend your life in rebellion against everyone and everything. And we wonder why depression, suicidal impulses, and sociopathic behavior are so common. It is simply not possible to live in a state of what secularists call "freedom."

Defining the Reality of Foolishness

And so they become fools. Everyone defines a fool a little differently but the real meaning of the word is the list in the three points above. Many writers claim these are not black and white issues. It is certainly true that foolishness has become like a smorgasbord for people who want to pick and choose what authority they will answer to, who they will be responsible to, and what beliefs and actions they are willing to accept consequences for. The simple truth, however, is that if you believe you are above any authority, and if you believe you have no responsibility, and if you think your beliefs and actions have no consequences, *you are a fool.*

Part One: Putting the Fear of God Into Your Writing

Positive Picture of Fearing God

So how does God set out to teach us to fear him? With a heavenly baseball bat? That's what secularists want you to believe, and that's what they write. The answer is the opposite. Proverbs 1 presents an extraordinarily positive picture of learning to fear God. It's how you begin to learn. There's no downside to absorbing scriptural teaching. You are never too old or too young to benefit. You are never too mature or immature.

Lifelong Instruction

Parental teaching, for example, can be lifelong instruction, even if it's only memories after parents are gone, that always gives protection and rewards. The wise will only get wiser. Your understanding will grow greater and greater. You'll become more disciplined. Righteousness, justice, and right living will become easier to practice. Best of all, you don't have to be afraid for your spiritual safety. People might be struck by judgment all around you, but they are the wicked. You are safe. (3:25)

Constant Protection

Do not abandon her [wisdom], and she will protect you. Love her, and she will watch over you. (4:6) Rather than threatening or frightening us, as you would expect, and as the world wants us to think, God extends another promise of protection.

Purity Promoted

Above everything else guard your heart, because from it flow the springs of life. (Proverbs 4:23, ISV) Don't let the words of the wicked sink into your heart and pollute your wellspring. Keep it pure.

Look at how Wisdom looks at God and at us in Proverbs 8.

> *Then I was with him, his master craftsman—I was his delight daily, continuously rejoicing in his presence, rejoicing in his inhabitable world and taking delight in mankind.* (Proverbs 8: 30-31, ISV)

Being with God is cause for rejoicing. Stop listening to those who say worship is boring. And remember that Wisdom personifies an attribute of God. So God takes delight in his human creation as well. There is blessing in waiting for God, in listening to Him, and there is life and favor.

Positive Rewards for Pursuing Wisdom

Of course we live in a sinful world, with the secular influence growing stronger and stronger, so things will not go perfectly. But they will go worse when we d*espise wisdom and discipline.* (1:7b, ISV)

Proverbs 2:5 is the culmination of the source of wisdom. Search with all your might for these great things and you'll fetch up against the fear of God and learn to know Him. Once again, fearing God only brings benefits: wisdom, protection, pleasantness. No downside.

Beautiful Ornaments

The Word of God should be like jewelry and accessories. It should be on display, accenting and ornamenting your life. (3:3, 4:9) People want us to keep our religion to ourselves. They don't want books to be "preachy." What does that even mean? Proverbs 3 says what you get from finding wisdom and gaining understanding is better than silver, gold, and rubies. (3:14-15) Nothing worldly minds desire compares to that "preachy" stuff. Nothing.

Proverbs 3 piles on more benefits of serving God faithfully. Great advice is not easy to find in books today. Mostly we are overrun by people who want us to feel good about ourselves, not become good before God. The real secret is in 3:5 (ISV) *Do not depend on your own understanding*. Not only does God promise great things like long life (3:2) good reputation (3:4), healing (3:8), and abundant provision for abundant giving (3:10), He makes a way for us to keep on track toward that lifetime acquisition of wisdom.

Clear Pattern

Wisdom is of utmost importance, therefore get wisdom, and with all your effort work to acquire understanding. (4:7, ISV) No bullying. Gentle persuasion. and the very next verse adds to the promises. *Prize her and she will exalt you. Indeed, if you embrace her, she will honor you.* (4:8, ISV)

(4:19, ISV) *The path of the righteous is like the light of dawn that grows brighter until the full light of day.* Every day it's easier to see the right way. Don't give in to the lie that God is mysterious and distant and impossible to figure out. He's making a path to Him and it's getting clearer all the time as we follow his instruction. Wisdom is a leader, a guardian, and a comforter. (6:22)

> *The fear of the LORD is where wisdom begins, and knowing holiness demonstrates understanding. For because of me you will live a long life, and years will be added to your life.* (Proverbs 9:10-11, ISV)

This is a key verse to understanding true biblical standards. Without this pattern to follow you have no hope of becoming wise or understanding.

10:24 promises that the righteous will get what he desires. Scoffers look at good people who have bad things happen to them, who might keep on experiencing bad things all their lives, and say this verse is a lie. But they don't understand what it means to be righteous; to align human desire with God's. That is a complete game-changer.

Welcome Correction

Possibly the biggest hurdle to overcome for sinful man is to get over thinking that "everyone's entitled to his opinion." Proverbs 12 concentrates on accepting correction for wrong behavior. And not just accepting, but loving it, according to verse 1. You will gain favor and security from God. *The lifestyle of the fool is right in his own opinion, but wise is the man who listens to advice.* (12:15, ISV) Your opinion about chocolate versus vanilla ice cream may not matter, but you had better not take the attitude that your lifestyle can be whatever you want it to be. Be wise. Listen to advice; especially from God's Word.

14:27 promises a fountain of life and a way to avoid the *snares of death.* Many so-called inspirational, motivational, and self-help writers sincerely want to encourage their readers and give them hope. But only the fear of the Lord and the ability to gain wisdom from Him is a true source of life. People can't get it from a "positive mental attitude."

15:33 lays out a difficult promise for our me-oriented, special, center-of-the-universe secularist training to accept. *Before honor is humility.* This is a lesson repeated throughout the Scriptures. Give up self, ambition, and pride, and God will exalt you as an example of His righteousness.

> *But when you are invited, go and recline at the last place, so that when the one who has invited you comes, he may say to you, 'Friend, move*

> *up higher'; then you will have honor in the sight of all who are at the table with you.* (Luke 14:10, NASB)

To the world, God is cruel and unfair, harshly punishing any who step out of line from His arbitrary and autocratic rules. He is like any "other" god from the world's mythologies. Men cringe in terror or simply shake their heads in frustration because no one can know how to really be right with God. But look at the simple reality of how *iniquity is purged* in 16:6: *by mercy and truth.*

Positive Behavior Promoting Wisdom

Sexual Fidelity

This is as positive as teaching about adultery gets. *"Let your fountain be blessed and enjoy the wife of your youth. Like a loving deer, a beautiful doe, let her breasts satisfy you all the time. Be constantly intoxicated by her love."* (5:18-19) This is both explicit and personal, but it's nothing dirty. Explicit sex in books is not appropriate when it is for the purpose of arousing wrong passions. This is a description of how a man should treat his marriage and his wife. This is good passion and self-control.

Study Benefits

Proverbs 7:2 (ISV) says, *Guard my teaching as you do your eyesight.* You should no more let people hinder your study of the Word than you should let them give you a poke in the eye. Treat Wisdom like family. Not the world's dysfunctional un-family, but the people you love and can't live without. Traditional Jews made phylacteries and wrapped them onto their arms and foreheads, with some of the Word inside, so that it would always be with them. But don't just keep it on the outside. *Engrave them on the tablet of your heart.* (7:3, ISV)

Hear what Wisdom offers in Chapter 8: prudence, an understanding heart, truth. Wickedness is detestable to her. She is all justice, without a scrap of corruption or perversity, and full of discretion. There's no pushing the envelope with Wisdom. She doesn't see how close to the line of inappropriateness she can get.

Since marriage is a picture of our relationship to God, 12:4 emphasizes the importance of virtue. Be a crown to your husband or wife in real life, of course. Don't be cancer in your spouse's bones. In the same way, believers need to be a credit to the Lord and not cause His Name to be blasphemed by their behavior. Don't assume that your infidelity in either case is "just a mistake" and that you will be forgiven and restored. A married person in a drama once protested to the wronged spouse that the adulterous relationship "didn't mean anything." The spouse replied, "It meant something to me." God forgives, and so can people, but it's not as if there are, or should be, no consequences for infidelity.

Powerful Influence

Not only is Wisdom good for you, her influence on you makes you valuable to others. She has power. All kinds of officials do their jobs better with her help, making things better for their people. (8:15-16)

Even as you grow in wisdom, you will find that sharing it sometimes works and sometimes doesn't. Proverbs is full of verses like this one: *Don't rebuke a mocker or he will hate you. Rebuke a wise person, and he will love you.* (9:8, ISV) Some people you can't fix. Happily there are some you can have the privilege of making better. *Counsel a wise man, and he will be wiser still; teach a righteous man, and he will add to his learning.* (9:9, ISV)

The fruit of the righteous is a tree of life, and the one who wins people is wise. (11:30, ISV) Our potential as wise children of God is limitless. We can and will influence others for righteousness.

Never forget that you can be an influence for good. 12:24 says that we can be in control rather than subservient if we are diligent. Some historians dismiss the influence of the Jewish people on other cultures. Careful scholars have discovered evidence that they may be responsible for many advances in technology in the ancient world. They were craftsmen, supervisors, and high-raking officials in many cultures. God blesses those who are faithful with power and influence.

> *A person's anxiety weighs down his heart, but an appropriate word is encouraging. The righteous person is cautious with respect to his neighbor, but the lifestyle of the wicked leads them astray. In the pathway to righteousness there is life, and in that lifestyle there is no death.* (12:25-26, 27, ISV)

We can be encouraging to those who are fearful and worried. There is a man living in Australia near a cliff where many people come to commit suicide. He invites people to his house "for tea and a chat." How many lives has he saved in that way? Many.

We can also let our example shine with righteousness instead of leading our neighbors into sin. And this is critical, if we have any hope of seeing them gain eternal life.

14:26 promises *strong confidence*. Humans need to stop writing about relying on "inner strength" or self-confidence, which is often nothing but pride. We need to give up the delusion that we have strength in ourselves.

Part Two: Pushing the Foolishness Out of Your Writing

Sinners Destroy Others

Blinding to the Obvious

If sinners entice you, do not consent. (1:11) Okay, Lord, tell us something we don't know. Stay away from bad guys. Why is this even in the Bible? If we are such know-it-alls, what is a sinner, and why is this not at all obvious? What could be more clear? Why would we want to *lie in wait for blood?* How could anyone entice us to be bloodthirsty? Why would God warn us about something so obvious?

Insensitivity Toward Death

Three examples show why it's not obvious. *First,* try convincing any random person that abortion is murder. Unless they already believe it, you will want to strangle them over the stupid and senseless answers they give. Babies are murdered by the garbage bag full, daily, and few people understand that they are humans worthy of protection. Even those who agree that normally it's wrong want exceptions. Why do rape and incest make it okay to kill the baby? They don't. The mother's life being in danger is still not a good reason to kill the baby. Which life is more important? We don't know how to choose.

Second, try convincing people that "mercy" killing or euthanasia of the supposedly terminally ill, the elderly, or the "brain dead" is a bad thing. Most people are so hammered by the culture of perfection that they don't even want to think about the withered, the comatose, or the otherwise imperfect. Only the perfect really have dignity, so, obviously, anything less must be terminated so that dignity is preserved.

Miserliness Toward Need

Do we even know what dignity means anymore? No, not when we think the helpless are better off dead. We blather about better use of resources like we're tossing an old car on a junk heap, not killing a person. This is where the passage gets to the nitty-gritty of *lying in wait for blood.* We "conserve resources" by not caring for the helpless. More *stuff* for us, in other words.

The basis of communism is supposed to be sharing the wealth equally, regardless of who worked to earn it. This is twisting the biblical principle of generosity. If he won't share, we get to take it from him, and if we have to kill him, he deserves to die for being so greedy.

Chapter 3 warns us against common practices in today's self-centered culture. *Don't withhold good.* (3:27) Pay off a debt as quickly as you can, rather than holding onto the money and forcing your creditor to come collecting. (3:28) Don't be part of the lawsuit-happy culture. (3:30)

Misinterpretation of Success

Third, our society is engaged in a feeding frenzy of self-enrichment. People honestly believe winning the lottery is the American dream. People have been murdered, endless lawsuits filed, deaths not reported, all to secure a winning ticket.

Organized crime is the darling of the secularist docudrama, because The Mafia, or *La Cosa Nostra,* has unbreakable codes of conduct, unparalleled interpersonal skills, and relentless drive to succeed. There's so much to admire; so much we can learn from crime families, Italian and otherwise. And every so-called good-guy in the movies and books ends up using the same tactics, stooping to the same bloodthirstiness, so it must be inescapable. Working purely for personal gain and ruthlessly destroying everything in opposition to your goals is the right thing to do.

Misdirecting Energy

Chapter 2, verse 12 begins a passage that gives us a choice. Secularists tell us we just have to do the best we can and overcome adversity by our human efforts, but God's promise is clear. We *can* be protected if we just seek wisdom. People scoff at this and point to a lifetime of bad stuff happening to good people. But remember that this life is not all there is. They don't want you to believe that. But the best part about serving God is that your spirit is protected, no matter what happens to your body.

Attacking Belief

For they cannot sleep unless they are doing evil, and they are robbed of their sleep unless they cause someone to stumble. (4:16) What an indictment! We have got to avoid the lawlessness, the self-indulgence the world teaches. It leads to the kind of thinking described in this verse: a hypercritical spirit, restlessness in the soul, and relentless attacks against others, often those who practice godliness. Why do secularists write book after book attacking Christianity? If there's no God, why do atheists waste so much time throwing roadblocks in front of believers? Insomnia from being on the wrong path.

Attacking Innocence

The seven signs of a sinner have been redefined in secularist literature, and even in that which is called Christian (6:16-19). Arrogance becomes self-confidence, lying becomes necessary control of information, hands shedding innocent blood is, of course "pro-choice," among other things. One example of a *heart crafting evil plans* is when people justify destroying the business or reputation of competitors or political adversaries by claiming to be better able to serve customers or "the people." "It wasn't personal. It was just business," says Tom Hanks in the movie *You've Got Mail,* channeling *The Godfather*. A big bookstore can sell books cheaper than a little one. So you destroy the little bookstores to help people get cheaper books, and, oh, by the way, enrich yourself.

Feet running swiftly to wickedness is the nonstop urge to accumulate more money, more power, more superiority over others. False witnesses always justify lying somehow. In the Scriptures, people testified against Nabal so that Jezebel could have him killed and get Ahab is vineyard. False witnesses also testified against Christ. These were both considered "for the good of the state" lies, believe it or not. Sometimes these people are threatened, and sometimes they are rewarded, to secure their testimony. The motivation is almost always selfish.

Attacking Family

Sowing quarrels among brothers has a modern parallel in the "dysfunctional family" lie that is hammered into our society through the media, entertainment and news. Families are under attack. Every effort is made to divide them. Younger siblings, instead of being nurtured and protected by older siblings, are shown as spoiled and receiving preferential treatment. School children are urged to tell troubles and wrongs to teachers and counselors rather than family members. They are also encouraged to inform against their families. "Are there guns in your house? Does that scare you?" "Do your parents force you to go to church, where you are made to feel sad or dirty or guilty?" Child abuse is a favorite construct of secularists, and it has grown from its origins in terrible realities to insanely broad concepts to twist children's thinking against their parents.

Older children are barraged with temptations to isolate themselves and rebel against family unity. Fathers are depicted as stupid, so boys have no role models. Sexual license fractures households where most of the children have different parents.

Teens form bonds with people who care about nothing but themselves. A drug supplier or sex partner becomes a friend because he or she keeps coming around and is willing to spend time with you. There is little loyalty or unity among modern siblings when it is torn away and given to those outside the home who are anything but worthy.

This is of not to say that children, or adults for that matter, should not have friends. David loved Jonathan as his own soul, more, he says, than the love men have for a wife. But look at Jonathan's character. Intelligent, skilled, courageous, righteous, selfless. Pick those kinds of friends.

Attacking Purity

The subject of "lovers" being misconstrued as friends also applies to adultery and fornication, whether it's pulling you away from siblings or not. The adulteress in Chapter 7 seems lonely, right? Her husband won't be back for a month, and if he took *a fistful of cash* (7:20, ISV) he's not going to miss his poor little wife. *"Let's comfort ourselves with love,"* she urges. This scenario really only has one ending. Here it is:

> *All of a sudden he follows her like an ox fit for slaughter or like a fool fit for a trap until an arrow pierces his liver. As a bird darts into a snare, he doesn't realize his fatal decision.* (7:22-23, ISV)

The world tells us that sexual sin is not that big of a deal. "Boys will be boys," said the officials in India when two teenaged girls were gang-raped and hanged from a neighborhood tree. Seriously. That was one of the answers villagers got when they demanded arrests and prosecutions.

> *Don't be led astray by her lifestyle, and don't imitate her behavior. For many are the victims whom she has conquered, and many are her slain. Her house leads to Sheol, descending to death's catacombs.*
> (7:25-27, ISV)

Proverbs 9 closes by contrasting the call of Wisdom with the call of the foolish woman. You might have gotten the impression that Wisdom was loud and annoying, but she's got nothing on this woman. The foolish woman is *loud, undisciplined, and without knowledge.* (9:13,ISV)

Stolen waters are sweet, and food eaten in secret is delicious, she says. (9:17, ISV) Does this just mean that she is a thief, and the meal she offers you is more exciting because it is stolen? Perhaps it means more, though. She could be referring to stealing what belongs to his rightful love, existing or future, and likely is speaking about oral sex. This is a common technique of prostitutes to avoid pregnancy. And having to hide a sexual relationship just makes it that much more "delicious," as the world is happy to tell you. People who engage in illicit sex seldom consider the possibility that their future holds what the next verse describes, though. *But he does not realize that the dead lurk there, and her invited guests wind up in the depths of Sheol.* (9:18, ISV)

Sinners destroy themselves by self-deception

Wisdom Does Not Lie Within

Wisdom's warning is clear. "Ignore me at your peril. At some point you're going to need me." Everyone does need wisdom to avoid distress and destruction. But she will laugh at you if you've ignored her all your life and suddenly try to sign up for a crash course. It doesn't work that way, but requires lifelong application and study.

Some writers claim to have wisdom from within themselves, or to gain it from other religions or teachers. You can't get it anywhere else. It doesn't come from opening your mind and emptying your thoughts. You can't climb a mountain, sit in a cave, or listen to someone else who sat under a tree and received enlightenment, and expect wisdom to come to you.

Sin Must Have Consequences

The fact that sinners destroy themselves should be obvious. But secularists have gotten pretty good at hiding or removing the consequences of sin. We are not allowed to ask if a person has a deadly, potentially contagious disease because we are invading his privacy. Deadly criminals wear the faces of children as pictures from their birthday parties are paraded in the media. Past crimes are frequently suppressed at trials because they could "prejudice" a jury. We are to assume all convictions are unjust, never punish anyone, and pity anyone "railroaded to justice."

Sinful Habits Must Be Broken

Hard truths are easy to find if you want to look. AIDS is much more common among homosexual males because their sinful habits are self-destructive. People who can't stop committing crimes expose themselves to capture. Prison culture foments drug abuse, self-mutilation, violence, and perverted conduct. Inmates are routinely injured or killed because they are so consumed with selfishness that they paradoxically expose themselves to more risks trying to "better" their position.

Sexual Temptation Must Be Resisted

Imagine being *completely* delivered from sexual sin. (Ch. 2:16 ff) That's what the adulteress is, you know. Sexual sin is the most mammoth temptation humans can face.

Some say Adam sinned because he chose Eve over God. Marriage is a covenant that pictures our relationship with God. Idolatry and adultery are really the same thing. Forsake your wife, forsake God. Don't do it. That "other woman" has done the same thing to her spouse and her God.

> *The strange woman, even from the stranger which flattereth with her words; Which forsaketh the guide of her youth, and forgetteth the covenant of her God.*
> (Proverbs 2:16-17)

And what's the reward you get for sexual sin? A front row seat in the *realm of the dead.* (2:18) *None who go to her return, nor do they reach the paths of life.* (2:19)

Back to that adulteress. She seems sweet, honey-tongued, *smooth as oil* (5:3) She's poison, though. She's a sword with two edges. Whichever way you turn, you're dead. (5:4) *You aren't thinking about where her life is headed; her steps wander, but you do not realize it.* (5:6, ISV) So many books toy with immorality but stop short of the actual act. They tease and tease but say there's nothing wrong as long as they don't "do the deed." The New Testament makes it clear that wrong thoughts are sins, too. Don't go close. Stay far away. It will cost you honor, strength, prosperity, and control. *You will cry out in anguish when your end comes when your flesh and body are consumed.* (5:11, ISV) Don't be that guy. Don't hate instruction. Listen. Take correction. Don't say it's boring. Don't say it's too much work.

We all know it would be stupid for a man to *scoop fire into his bosom.* When was the last time anyone thought of adultery that way? Burn your clothes? That's the least of it! But you can't even get people to be that sensible. Not even church people. Secularists laugh at the legions of pastors and church secretaries who run off together, or don't even run off. *Anyone touching her will not remain unpunished,* (6:29, ISV) by God, if by no one else.

Let's go back to the days when *any* sex outside of marriage was wrong, okay? Can we do that? People have such a casual attitude toward sex. Around the world, children, men, and women just take what they want; everything from little ones in daycare going way beyond "playing doctor," to preteens sexting, to teens pulling swimsuits off in the pool, to adults swinging from partner to partner, all the way to those who gang rape or have orgies.

> *He* (the adulterer) *will receive a beating and dishonor, and his shame won't disappear, Jealousy incites a strong man's rage, and he will show no mercy when it's time for revenge.* (Proverbs 6:33-34, ISV)

Violence Must Not Be Gratuitous

Violence is not cool. That doesn't mean you should be a pacifist or an anti-war demonstrator. The Scriptures say, *Cursed is the one who is slack in doing the Lord's work. Cursed is the one who holds back his sword from shedding blood.* (Jeremiah 48:10, ISV) Wars for the right reason are necessary. Don't despise soldiers because you think *thou shalt not kill* means never, ever, for any reason. It means "do no murder."

Our society creates confusion regarding protection by force, including military service. On the one hand we are told to honor soldiers, and on the other hand told to stop letting them kill and be killed doing the job of defending freedom. "Bring our boys home" trumps letting them defend against the imprisonment, robbing, and slaughter of people who want and need to be free of oppression by evil.

What we should not do is revel in the latest dirt on actors and musicians who glorify rape and abuse, associate themselves with gangs, destroy their hotel rooms. These things are *not* admirable. (3:31)

Many books glorify lurid violence; graphic, horrible descriptions of serial killings and other perverted crimes. Why do you want to read 300 pages of gory monstrous inhumanity and maybe 100 about the good guy trying to catch him? And what if the hero is "forced" to be violent, profane, and lewd himself? Books love to sully reputations and ruin character to solve a crime. *Indeed, a perverse man is utterly disgusting to the LORD, but he takes the upright into his confidence.* (3:2) Don't seek out books that pervert what a hero should be.

Marriage Must Be Protected

Husbands, can you try to be that strong man who shows no mercy to the man who wants your wife? Wives, can you make your man love you and keep him at home? Can you rekindle a flame and be loving and lovable? Obviously we can't always overcome the unrepentant sin nature. But jealousy is not always wrong. Being constantly suspicious with no cause can destroy a marriage, but so can weakness and failing to be the person, man or woman, who does not love a spouse enough to hate infidelity and put a stop to it. Make an adulterer or adulteress ashamed. Do what it takes to save your marriage.

Fornication Leads to Death

An adulteress can tempt a single guy, too, and the same applies to a married man going after single women. Don't dismiss the adulteress as a misogynist concept and therefore irrelevant. A universal principle can be illustrated by a limited example. The *senseless young man* of Proverbs 7:7 is the "how could I be such an idiot" of today, male or female, who is seduced by a married person. That *brazen and defiant* (7:11) person is *intending to entrap him* [or her] (7:10).

I've come out to meet you, I've looked just for you, and I found you! (7:15, ISV) Flattery is a great seducer. "You are so special. You're exactly what I was looking for." *She leads him astray with great persuasion; with flattering lips she seduces him.* (7:21, ISV)

> *A thief isn't despised if he steals to meet his needs when he is hungry, but when he is discovered, he must restore seven-fold, forfeiting the entire value of his house.*
> (Proverbs 6:30-31, ISV)

Those who practice seduction take prisoners, steal food, destroy lives (6:25 ff) Adultery is playing with fire. It's not cute and funny as it's so often depicted. It's certainly not justified by a busy or uninterested or disabled spouse. Yet these are the messages screamed at us by sitcoms and dramas, that infidelity is entertaining and to be winked at. Here's the truth. *Whoever commits adultery with a woman is out of his mind; by doing so he corrupts his own soul.*
(6:32, ISV)

Sin Corrupts

Theft Has a Price

Many, many books present the helpless poor person who will die if he doesn't steal a loaf of bread. Of course this is reality. No one is denying that such people exist. People didn't "poach upon the king's deer" in the Robin Hood tales because it was fun to be mutilated or killed. They did it because they needed to eat, all the land belonged to the king, and he was the only one who could legally hunt on thousands of acres. Throughout time oppression has driven people to steal for food. But the law is the law, and if a person is caught, he will pay, fair or not fair. Secularists need to stop being screaming social activists trying to overthrow all law and control so that everybody has to share everything until no one has anything left and we're all trying to beg or steal to live.

Lies and Vulgarity Corrupt

Never talk deceptively and don't keep company with people whose speech is corrupt. (4:24) So many books play havoc with truth. They exalt a clever liar and a silver-tongued deceiver. The more vulgar the speech the bigger the admiration, because it makes the characters seem real. Potty language, profanity, all kinds of spew are even included in the works of believers to get unbelievers to feel comfortable with reading the book. Really? We want unbelievers to feel *uncomfortable,* because of something called *conviction.* We want to be better than the world, and give it a better example, not see how close we can come to what they say and do so they'll like us better and read our books.

> *The wicked person's iniquities will capture him, and he will be held with the cords of his sin. He will die for lack of discipline, and he goes astray because of his great folly.*
> (Proverbs 5:22-23, ISV)

Foolishness and lack of self-control are fatal. They are not little things. They are big things, with big consequences. Don't be captured by things that will hog-tie you and kill you because you have listened to the world teach you that you have rights and freedoms. In sexual matters, you don't.

The Lord warns us about things that He hates in the latter part of Chapter 6. Have you noticed the weird gestures of many musicians? What do they mean? They make us think of *winking with his eyes, making signs with his feet, pointing with his fingers.* (6:13, ISV) The Lord describes these as devious people. Our culture perverts music, speech, and thereby understanding .

Rebellion Is Self-Endangerment

Proverbs 8 ends with a warning after giving heaps of positive reasons to stick with God. *But whoever sins against me destroys himself; everyone who hates me loves death.* (8:36, ISV)

In the previous section much time is given to establishing the fact that God does not hate us. God loves us. God wants what is best for us. But some people are extremely stubborn and require an easier way to understand the fear of God and the consequences of failing to develop it. So imagine God as the king of beasts, the lion. Once you get a lion angry, there's not much you can do but run. You are putting yourself in extreme danger. It's not the lion's fault if you get eaten. The same is true of God and sin. At some point, He has to judge sin. People who sin and do not repent are wronging themselves; putting themselves in danger. *The fear of a king is as the roaring of a lion: whoso provoketh him to anger sinneth against his own soul.* (20:2)

Sinners Ignore Wisdom

Not only do they ignore wisdom, they hate it, and consistently choose against it. (1:29) Who is that annoying woman demanding your attention? She's called wisdom. What does she want from you? Nothing. She wants to give you *everything*. Well, she does want one thing. She wants you to *listen.*

Dangers of Trusting Self

Possibly the most enormous wrong writers do to their readers is to tell them they are special, unique, have a divine spark, should follow their hearts, and that they have innate wisdom and need not listen to anyone.

No Guidance

The rest of Chapter 1 lays out dire consequences for not listening to wisdom. Yes, you have the freedom to ignore her. But there will come a point at which you will want her, and she will reject you. *Indeed, the waywardness of the naïve will kill them, and the complacency of fools will destroy them.* (1:32, ISV)

But the way of the wicked is like deep darkness, and they do not know what they are stumbling over. (4:19, ISV) In contrast to the path of the righteous, this one just keeps getting harder to follow. Darker, more treacherous. Why are they so determined to go that way?

No Safety

This is what makes this position so stupid. Why are they ignoring wisdom? Is it because she is bad for them? Something worse will happen than being killed and destroyed? *But the person who listens to me will live safely and will be secure from the fear of evil.* (1:33, ISV) Sounds pretty good to me. Not something to ignore at all.

Cruelty is overwhelmingly common in modern society and is becoming more and more accepted. People deflect attention from the horrors perpetrated against human beings by posting pictures of abused dogs. Michael Vick will never be forgiven for the dogfights. But it's hard to get people to even understand, much less care, that all over the world people are kidnapped, tortured, imprisoned, and have their property and places of worship vandalized, stolen, or destroyed because they are Christians. We are either distracted by puppy and elephant pictures or told those people had a choice and could just convert to the religion of their country or leave.

Being faithful to your religion means nothing to secularists anyway. And they don't tell you that to "just leave" these people must surrender property, possessions, everything except the clothes they are allowed to wear. They must submit to invasive, sometimes brutal searches to make sure they are not hiding any valuables. Their vehicles are stolen and they are forced to walk through desert terrain without food or water until someone assists them.

The number of ways people justify Hamas daily firing rockets into Israel from Palestine is staggering. They can do it a thousand times, but if Israel fires back once, that is considered cruelty. "Peace will come when the Arabs will love their children more than they hate us." Hamas built miles of concrete-reinforced tunnels to attack the Jews and not a single bomb shelter. Weapons are stored at schools and hospitals. If the Palestinians complain about being used as human shields, they are shot. These are examples of true cruelty. Yet the world calls it fighting for freedom.

Dangers of Trusting Finances

No Self-Control

Chapter 6 urges us not to fall into the credit culture trap. How many books have you read where people swipe a card for things they cannot wait and save up for? One movie, *Regarding Henry,* had a woman sharing with a friend that because of her husband's catastrophic injury they were in serious financial trouble. The friend's advice was to run all their credit up to the maximum. The woman, wisely, chose to reduce instead, letting go a housekeeper and moving to a less expensive home. If you do have to borrow, pay it back as quickly as possible. Lose sleep if you have to. Don't be a chronic debtor.

Lots of books, fiction and non-fiction, are written about investing, too. That may be the best application for *if you guarantee a loan for your neighbor, if you have agreed to a deal with a stranger* (6:1, ISV). People who wheel and deal with loans, investments, stocks, and things along those lines are considered admirable. They are exciting risk-takers but often they lack moral perspective. Do not seek to be like them.

No Security

What does an ant really do that we have to try to emulate? It plans ahead. It prepares for the future. (6:6) Other Scriptures say don't boast about tomorrow, and don't think you've made yourself prosperous and can now take it easy. But it's wisdom to save and store up, within reasonable limits.

No Generosity

Don't forget to be generous and don't refuse to help when legitimate needs arise. The Scriptures say over and over that God promises to be generous with us so we can be generous with others. (See Section 2 for examples of this from the Book of Numbers)

Look at what Wisdom did for us in Proverbs 9. She built a house, prepared a feast, and invited us in to enjoy ourselves with her. She only asks one thing in return. *Leave your naïve ways, and live. Walk in the path of understanding.* (9:6, ISV) But how many people say believers in God are naïve? How many scoff at the very idea that God could be loving and welcoming and offering us a feast along with eternal life?

No Spirituality

Many of the chapters from 10 on forward present the see-sawing choices humans can make. Will you be wise or will you be foolish? Bring joy or bring sorrow? Will you allow the Lord to provide bountifully for you or suffer cravings that can't be satisfied and shouldn't be indulged? You can work hard or you can be a disgrace. Your words can be choice silver or insignificant.

> *What the wicked fears will come about, but the longing of the righteous will be granted. When the storm ends, the wicked vanish, but the righteous person is forever firm.*
> (10:24-25, ISV)

Secularists will tell you that having or living a good life has nothing to do with serving God. They are making up their own standards for integrity, however. And they disagree with each other. Some of the conditions set up in this chapter seem unrealistic, and people who deny God are quick to point out that the faithful often remain in poverty, have troubles, and die young. This is true. God sends His rain on the just and the unjust. And sin has spillover effects on everyone. The point is to have the right attitude and to understand spiritual success and our future with God. The wicked are quick to assign blame to God when bad things happen. Their prophecies are sometimes self-fulfilling. Righteousness has eternal value.

> *The words of the righteous overflow with wisdom, but the perverse tongue will be cut out. Righteous lips know what is prudent, but the words of the wicked are perverse.*
> (Proverbs 10: 30-31, ISV)

No Trust

Many common practices in society today divide and isolate people by destroying trust. Chapter 11 lists many behaviors that give secularists a field day in interpreting them. False scales are the delight of the wicked. They insist we should not judge, but they are always judging by a false standard, with pride, hypocrisy, and attempts to corrupt. *The treacherous are trapped by their evil desires.* (11:6, ISV) Sometimes these divisive efforts are successful, as they play on the frailty of fallen man. Our only hope is to let God give us the means of escape. *By what he says, the godless person can destroy his neighbor, but through knowledge the righteous escape.* (11:9, ISV)

No Fellowship

Belittling, gossip, ruthlessness, cruelty, lack of discretion ... These are obvious sins that the modern world tries to redefine. Sitcoms rely on making viewers see themselves as better than those losers on the show. Gossip is just caring about others enough to share our concerns with a few dozen close friends. Ruthlessness is considered determination to succeed.

Like a gold ring in a pig's snout is a beautiful woman without discretion. (11:22, ISV) To be without discretion is to seek sexual attention. Little girls are dressed like whores and have no conception of modesty. They may have sparkles and lace and bright jewels but it's making them into pigs. All this goes right along with loud, rude, uncontrolled behavior. Seeking attention is essential for girls who have been told since infancy that they are beautiful, special, and deserve to be the center of attention. They don't understand why the only kind of attention they get now is the wrong kind. This applies to boys and young men as well.

The latter part of Chapter 11 details the contrast between generosity and greed. Generosity results in plenty for yourself. Withholding what people need isn't considered being thrifty. It will get you a curse. A person who trusts in his wealth will fail because wealth is temporary. *The person seeking good will find favor, but anyone who searches for evil—it will find him!* (1:27, ISV) This also applies to the things you spend time on. You don't need to explore every possible evil to know how to combat it. You will just be inviting more evil into your mind and heart, because it's so addictive.

Sinners want to sell you a get-rich-quick scheme. Even megachurch pastors want you to follow a gospel of wealth. Maybe it's true that many people in the Scriptures, Old and New Testaments, were wealthy, and therefore had more freedom to serve God. The Scriptures, however, do not promote wealth as a necessity, either to prove that you are right with God or to enable you to serve God to the fullest. The fear of the

Lord is the only component essential to heartfelt service. *Better is little with the fear of the LORD than great treasure and trouble therewith.* (Proverbs 15:16, ISV)

Part Three -- Proceeding With Caution

Books sometimes have things in them that are bad. We object to them. But that does not mean the book itself is bad. This final section will deal with objectionable elements, and give some insights from Proverbs about the biblical perspective we should have. We need to learn to discern when to toss a book and when to hold our nose and learn what it can still teach us that is valuable.

Bad Language

Keep in mind that the Bible contains things that were considered profanity, swearing, or vulgar language. Mostly these are spoken by bad guys, like the Rabshakeh threatening Hezekiah. Many other books contain more or less bad language.

Never talk deceptively and don't keep company with people whose speech is corrupt. Proverbs 4:24 (ISV) says that the most important thing about speech is that it be truthful. So, in the example of the Rabshakeh, he doesn't get a pass for talking that way because his purpose was to demoralize and create disloyalty in the hearts of the Israelites. He told them the true God was no different than the false gods who couldn't stop the conquest of the people who worshiped them. The Rabshakeh thought one god was no different from another. So he was speaking deceptively, and his speech was corrupt in the language he used and his intentions. Learn to identify and avoid the teaching of the bad guys who rely on bathroom talk and other kinds of foul language and lie to destroy your confidence and make you afraid.

Kings take pleasure in righteous speech; they treasure a person who speaks what is upright. (16:13,ISV) This is the flip side of bad speech. The Rabshakeh tried to "reach out to the common man" in his speech, pretending he was just trying to help them out. He said Hezekiah was not doing right by them. But his lies didn't work, because Hezekiah knew the value of righteous speech. He went to his King, the Lord, in prayer, with honesty and true humility.

Sexual Sin

For the lips of an adulteress drip honey, and her speech is smoother than oil. (5:3) Do you lower your standards for entertainment? Do you let the lure of romance seduce you into thinking it's okay to read unmarried or otherwise illicit explicit sex? Do you say, "It's only fiction?" Do you give all that adultery, fornication, and explicit detail a pass because some bad guy gets made better by a good woman and it has a happy ending?

Do you read vampire romances? Do you know the meaning of the word *necrophilia*? It means having sex with the dead. Can you explain how a vampire romance is *not* necrophilia? There are stories now that don't even pretend to talk about the "undead." They have people getting married to the dead. And they are marketed to young audiences and called "cute" and "sweet". Anything goes, as long as there's a happy ending and romance. Maybe they don't even contain explicit detail, but the clear message is that perversion is okay if it's tender, funny, and you can squint and crook your neck and bend over backwards to find a good message in there somewhere.

Do you read werewolf romances? Do you know what the word *bestiality* means? The Scriptures condemn sex with an animal. These works also open the door to multiple partners, another form of fornication. A romance label slapped on a book does not give you the freedom to fill your head with things the Scriptures clearly condemn.

Are you one who *loves purity and gracious speech*? (22:11, ISV) You will not find such things in these kinds of books.

Do you allow for homosexuality in what you read? You've read a book or watched a TV show, probably, with a sympathetic guy who is every girl's shopping buddy, best friend, and confidant, because he's safe. He's not going to break your heart. He's not interested in you "that way." Gay men are becoming so common in romantic comedies that you would think half the males in America were gay.

Estimates vary, but the reality from the CDC, as they investigated STDs, is that maybe 3% of the population might be homosexual, male or female. These characters *crowd* these stories for the express purpose of altering your perceptions about the nature of love. There can be all kinds of love, right? All of it, once the misunderstandings are worked out, is lighthearted, fun, and feel-good. Or maybe it's a serious story and they share a dangerous quest. So what if it's two men, or two women? Are you saying they aren't entitled to happiness?

Lesbians are pretty common in books nowadays, too, and have been for longer than men. They usually figure in more "serious" books, sandwiched in with terrifying crimes or government corruption or radiation threats. The issues of these works are so "important" that you have to read them, and give the lesbian relationship a pass. There are serious books including gay relationships, too. You are not allowed to say that the relationship is reprehensible when the topic of the book is so vitally important.

Here's why you shouldn't give a pass to homosexuality. *The fear of the LORD is to hate evil. Pride, arrogance, an evil lifestyle, and perverted speech I despise.* (8:13, ISV) In numerous places, the Bible condemns homosexuality. Nobody's misinterpreting those verses except the justifiers of this perversion. The Scriptures say what they say and they mean it's "an evil lifestyle." Pride and arrogance make people say Scripture doesn't mean what it means. This is perverted speech, for a perverted purpose.

Violence

We've already spent some time talking about excessive violence, but here are a few more thoughts. Some people are more willing to keep reading a book with lots of violence than any other element they might normally object to. The Bible has lots of violence, and some of it is pretty depraved and gruesome. But is it described in detail? And is it presented as something to admire and emulate? Do you want to go out and rip up pregnant women or smash the heads of babies against rocks after reading about it in the Bible? *Bloodthirsty men hate the innocent person, but the upright show concern for his life.* (29:10,ISV) God clearly spells out the punishment for people who commit these atrocities in other Scriptures and shows that He does not desire these horrors. Nor does He dwell on them. The books you read or write should not, either.

The words of the wicked lead to bloodshed, but the speech of the upright delivers them. (12:6, ISV) Is it edifying to read a book that presents many violent acts described in detail? Mentions of violence in the Bible, like all the other objectionable elements, are relatively brief and contain little detail. Sometimes it is necessary to talk about violence, but it can be presented in a way that spares the reader pain and spiritual harm to the extent possible. *A gentle statement is a tree of life, but perverted speech shatters the spirit.* (15:4, ISV)

Two concepts that many people wrongly think of as being the same thing are fantasy and the occult. Fantasy is a broad term including even stories that are completely realistic, except that they take place in an imaginary location. They can also go completely to the other end of the spectrum where anything and everything can be controlled by magic of various kinds.

People need discernment to understand the difference between fantastic literature, which can be harmless and even edifying, and that which gives too much place to the occult, or forces that have evil, dark spiritual, and dangerous origins. *To the LORD evil plans are detestable, but pleasant words are pure.* (15:26, ISV) The Lord hates those who ensnare people with seductive powers that lead to death. But He loves those who communicate pleasant, pure words.

Consider the source of the material. The Scriptures say that the innocent (we are defining innocent as obtaining righteousness from Christ) have the potential to make a path that is level, or good, to follow. *The righteousness of the innocent creates a level path, but the wicked fall by their wickedness.* (11:5, ISV) So, if the source of the writing is a believer who seeks to be obedient, the work is unlikely to contain dangerous occult content. At the very least, it will be clearly defined as evil and presented as something to be avoided and fought against.

Consider that even a believer might be deceived about his own ability to present pure words. *Everything a person does seems pure in his own opinion.* Remember that *the LORD weighs intentions.* (16:2, ISV) Any writing must be weighed by God through prayer and study of the Scriptures. It is so easy to get carried away by the story, both as a reader and a writer, and include things that should not be there. *Some people view themselves as pure, but haven't been cleansed from their own filth.* (30:12, ISV)

Many writers feel compelled to accurately and fully present evil so that readers will know how to combat it. Certainly the Scriptures present Satan himself and make His nature and danger to us clear, but if we were able to separate out the references to God and His goodness from those referring to Satan and his evil, there would not be equality or balance.

False Philosophical or Religious Assumptions

So many people line out the "big three" objections – language, sex, and violence, and forget all about the real underlying philosophy of a work. It might not have any real language, sex, or violence, but is still wrong because of what it teaches. The world wants man to have his own standards of right and wrong. Man wants to be the one who decides about good and evil. This is completely contrary to the way things have to be. God created everything, including our spiritual natures, and He alone knows how things have to operate. Adam and Eve had one rule to follow. Just one, that we know of, but they wanted to make their own decisions and chart their own destinies. Man has wanted that ever since, always with disastrous consequences.

Like a gold earring and a necklace of pure gold is a wise reprover to a listening ear. (25:12, ISV) Learn to submit to God's authority, and those who give good and godly counsel. It's like being rewarded, being decked out with jewels, to get a chance to hear wisdom telling us we've gone off the path.

It's not punishment. It should not make us angry and resentful. It's treasure. If a book is full of kids rebelling because they don't want to follow their parents' rules, that's a wrong philosophy. Some books set up the parents as cruel, excessively strict, even beating and locking up their kids. Remember that the author has a purpose in making those parents that way. In real life, such parents are rare, but in books, they are epidemic.

Human beings long for grace, and it's better to be poor than a man of deceit. (19:22,ISV) Look for books that point you toward the grace of God. They might tell you how to get rich, or be comfortable, or get along better with the world. But that's not what you need. That's a deceitful message, if it leaves out God and our absolute need to get closer to Him. Read books that help you stop shoving things in between yourself and God. We need to get riches and comfort and even other people out of the way so we can see Him better. *A fortune gained by deceit is a fleeting vapor and a deadly snare.* (21:6, ISV)

Popular culture teaches us to love and tolerate everyone, redefining those words to mean embrace sinful lifestyles. This is an extremely damaging philosophy. They teach that it is only right to hate people who disagree with loving and accepting everybody. *Someone who hates hides behind his words, harboring deceit within himself.* (26:24, ISV) The people who are the real haters hide behind "love" and "tolerance" and whip up hatred against people who don't agree with them. The term "-phobe" means fear, and this philosophy teaches that people only disagree with sin out of fear, because they are too ignorant to understand that there is no sin. No, we disagree with sin because God disagrees with it.

Many people today claim to be working for peace. They believe that is what everyone wants, and that the solution is to get rid of weapons and make agreements so that everybody has everything they need and no one has any reason to fight. Look at small children playing in a room full of toys. The odds are very good that one child will want a toy that another child is playing with.

There are many, many toys. But most people will say, "Oh, that child must share with the one who wants his toy." Why must he give up the toy he has, when the other child has many others to choose from? Some children will get in a fight over one toy. The need to possess something someone else has, or to hold on to what you already have, can overwhelm all other senses. Selfishness robs all people of all ages of the ability to think and make good decisions.

It is deceptive to think everything must, or even can, be equal, or equally shared. Peace can only be obtained by imposing outside rules. You are more likely to give things up than to share them, in a situation that brings real peace. Every set of rules demands sacrifices, but giving things up is essential when people live together. You give up the freedom to walk across a stranger's lawn because there is a law against trespassing. You pay for items you pick up in a store because there is a law against stealing.

People who teach that everybody has freedom and we can all get along if we just respect that are deceivers. *Deceit is at home in the heart of those who plan evil, but those who promote peace rejoice.* (12:20, ISV) Peace demands limitations. In the Scriptures, we are told there will be times when the wolf will lie down with the lamb, and a child will be able to play over a snake's hole. In order for that to happen, the wolf must give up eating lambs, and the snake must give up biting children.

Conclusion – The Perfect Standard from Ephesians 4

The Scriptures provide a perfect standard for all things. But we live in a sinful world, and among sinful people, so not everyone pays attention to the Scriptures. We have to be on our guard. Satan is the father of liars, and he trains his children throughout their lives to think wrong things so they can perform wrong actions. The lost, being deceived by the master deceiver, think they are undeceived. They think they have freedom, knowledge, and the ability to tell everyone else how to live. They have the farthest thing from the perfect standard.

The conduct of a guilty man is perverse, but the behavior of the pure is upright. (Proverbs 21:8, ISV) The world is guilty. We cannot afford to whitewash that, and say "so and so is a good person." We cannot say that if people do the best they can, everything will work out.

Egyptian mythology says that when a man dies, he will stand before Anubis, the god of the underworld, who has a set of scales. Anubis will place a feather on one side and the man's heart on the other. If the heart weighs more than the feather, the man is condemned. Many people go through life believing their good deeds will somehow outweigh their bad deeds, but this is another form of deception.

Thank God, we are not judged for eternal salvation on our works. No one is righteous. No one is even "good enough." And human standards are not good enough to judge what to read and what to write.

Look at Ephesians 4. In verse one, Paul says he will reveal to us the way to be worthy of our calling. So here comes the perfect standard.

vv. 2,3 *Demonstrating all expressions of humility, gentleness, and patience, accepting one another in love. Do your best to maintain the unity of the Spirit by means of the bond of peace.* (ISV)

Secularists might shout that this is exactly what they have been saying all along. You humble yourself before us, and accept and love everybody. Let's have unity, and then we'll have peace.

Do you see the picking and choosing that is going on here? They have skipped right over the most important criteria to have the right standard. The unity is only possible in the Spirit, that is, the Holy Spirit of God. He grants us discernment and teaches us the standard to follow, not the world. Everybody can't love everybody and be unified with everybody because not everybody has the Holy Spirit living inside them. One body and one spirit applies only to believers.

Nobody else gets to claim that kind of love and acceptance. This is not to say we shouldn't love and pray for the lost, even the most vile, but we cannot have unity with them. They are like the preschooler who grabs everyone else's toys, and with his arms so full he can't hold anymore, still wants to take away yours. "Love me, accept me, just as I am, or you're the one who's wrong!" secularists scream. But they don't share our Lord, our faith, or our baptism (the Holy Spirit). Our "toys" are the gifts from God our father, and cannot be shared with those who are not His children. His gifts are powerful. Here's what they do:

> *Equip the saints, to do the work of ministry, and to build up the body of the Messiah until all*

> *of us are united in the faith and in the full knowledge of God's Son, and until we attain mature adulthood and the full standard of development in the Messiah.*
> (Ephesians 4:12-13, ISV)

God gave man everything when He created him. But here's the best the world can do with the corrupted versions of the gifts they have retained since the fall, in their unregenerate, selfish, blind groping. *Tossed like waves and blown about by every wind of doctrine, by people's trickery, or by clever strategies that would lead us astray.* (Ephesians 4:14, ISV)

Here's what we have to do instead of letting the world tell us what to do, or even completely separating from it and letting it go its own way. It's not optional. We are the only chance the world has to see belief in action. We are salt and light. Yes, God gives the increase, but there is no question that we have to be the sowers and the waterers and the cultivators. But first, we have to clean up our own act as believers and supposed teachers of other believers.

> *Instead, by speaking the truth in love, we will grow up completely and become one with the head, that is, one with the Messiah, in whom the whole body is united and held together by every ligament with which it is supplied. As each individual part does its job, the body builds itself up in love.* (4:15-16, ISV)

Don't live like the Gentiles anymore, Paul shouts at us. Don't think *worthless thoughts.* (v. 17)

> *They are darkened in their understanding and separated from the life of God because of their ignorance and hardness of heart. Since they have lost all sense of shame, they have abandoned themselves to sensuality and*

> *practice every kind of sexual perversion without restraint.* (vv. 18-19, ISV)

You were taught, Paul says, a completely different way to come to the Messiah. *Strip off your old nature.* It was *being ruined by its deceptive desires.* (v. 22, ISV) This is what regeneration and rebirth is all about. This is the new creation in Christ. *Be renewed in your mental attitude, ...clothe yourselves with the new nature, which was created according to God's image in righteousness and true holiness.* (v. 24, ISV)

Strip off falsehood, Paul orders us. This is true "transparency," another word secularists love to redefine. "Trust me," they say endlessly, but you can't trust them. They still have the old nature. They are still deceived and wanting the wrong things. We have to speak truth with our neighbor, our fellow believer, because we belong in the same body, to Christ. No secrets. No lies. True transparency. True unity.

The rest of Chapter 4 is like an encapsulated answer to many of the issues brought up in other parts of this book. It's okay to get angry, in spite of the world crying "peace, peace." Just don't use anger as an excuse to sin. *Do not give the devil an opportunity to work.* (4:27, ISV) If you were a thief, you are forgiven, cleansed by the blood of Christ, just like any other forgiven sinner. Don't do it anymore. Work. Earn income, and learn to be generous so other people don't think they have to resort to stealing.

> *Let no filthy talk be heard from your mouths, but only what is good for building up people and meeting the need of the moment. This way you will administer grace to those who hear you.* (4:29, ISV)

The world doesn't need to see how close you can come to them. It needs to be shocked by how far away you are from them. They need to look up to you, to see Christ standing right behind you, at the top of those stairs that lead to glory. Don't grieve the Holy Spirit by going down there with them. Bring them up to Him. It's the only way you will be effective in service. Show people that mark, that seal of redemption. Don't hang your head and say they don't want to see it. They need to. They desperately need to.

But be careful that by demonstrating your separation, you do not give in to pride and become contemptuous of the lost. *Let all bitterness, wrath, anger, quarreling, and slander be put away from you, along with all hatred.* (v. 30, ISV)

Hate the sin, but love the sinner. Don't despise them. You once *were* them. Don't excuse or accept their sin, but love their soul. One pastor's wife created a ministry by offering meals to exotic dancers outside gentlemen's clubs. She didn't go in. She waited outside. She just offered them a hot meal, and a chance for more. *And be kind to one another, compassionate, forgiving one another just as God has forgiven you in the Messiah.* (v. 32, ISV)

Some say the context of these verses mean they apply to relationships between Christians, and there's no doubt that they do. Still, your conduct should be consistent, so it makes sense that you behave the same toward sinners as you do toward believers. Treat sin as sin, but show kindness and compassion. Remember that you have been forgiven, so give them a chance to experience God's forgiveness. Upon their repentance, you forgive them, and harbor no bitterness; engage in no slander.

So look for the right things to read, and write about the right things. When you see the bad things in books, know them for what they are and don't be afraid to point them out as such. Learn to discern. Learn the standards God teaches. Don't accept the world's teaching. That doesn't mean you're not allowed to read anything but the good stuff, but you had better know the difference, and not let secularism creep into your thinking as you read. Just as learning wisdom is a lifelong process, so being on your guard against devious ideas is as well.

References

Charron, Pierre. *De la sagesse* ("Of Wisdom," In Three Parts). French version, 1601. Translated by Samson Lennard, Eliot's Court Press for Edward Blount and Will, Aspley, London, c.1615.

Definition of choice from: http://www.oxforddictionaries.com/us/definition/american_english/choice

Golda Meir National Press Club Washington DC 1957

Dorothy L. Sayer, "The Other Six Deadly Sins," *Creed or Chaos,* Harcourt, Brace and Company, New York: NY, 1994, p. 81.

The best gift you can give an author

is an honest, thoughtful review. Please consider leaving one online. Help us understand what you liked and didn't like about the book and why. Help authors reach more readers and spread your influence and ours. If you liked the book, please recommend it to your spouse, friends, pastors, teachers, cashiers, employers, – anybody and everybody you see each day. If you don't know what to say, remember Proverb 16:3 – Commit thy works unto the Lord and thy thoughts shall be established. Thank you!

OTHER BOOKS AND PRODUCTS FROM FINDLEY FAMILY VIDEO PUBLICATIONS

All our books (including Historical Fiction, SciFi, contemporary relationships short stories, and an Archaeological Mystery serial) are linked on our blog.

Elk Jerky for the Soul includes posts on current issues, excerpts from our fiction and nonfiction works, Bible teaching, travel and everyday observations, and more.

http://findleyfamilyvideopublications.com/

Visit our YouTube Channel

https://www.youtube.com/channel/UCGhwNpU115ARMwgYwTIJBrA/featured. Book trailers, video excerpts, project teasers, and more. Science, History, Literature, and biblical worldview studies are the focus of our book and video projects.

Historical Fiction

by Michael J. Findley

The Ephron the Hittite Series (Including boxed set of all titles)

Ephron Son of Zohar

Tawananna Daughter of Zohar

Heth Son of Canaan Son of Ham, Noah

Shelometh Daughter of Yovov Wife of Ephron

Zita Son of Ephron and Shelometh

Adult Romantic Suspense

by Mary C. Findley

The Men of the Realmlands series

Book One: The Baron's Ring

Book Two: The Captain's Blade

Send a White Rose

Chasing the Texas Wind

Carrie's Hired Hand (novella)

Young Adult Historical Adventure

by Mary C. Findley

Hope and the Knight of the Black Lion (plus illustrated version)

The Benny and the Bank Robber Series

Benny and the Bank Robber (Plus homeschool editions for student and teacher with review and vocabulary)

Doctor Dad

The Oregon Sentinel

Lines in Pleasant Places

Science Fiction and Fantasy

by Michael J. Findley

The Empire Saga (all six of the following books in one volume)

City on a Hill and Sojourner (Combined Novella and Short Story)

Nehemiah LLC (Full-length novel available as a standalone ebook, paperback, and hardcover versions)

Empire One: Humiliation

Empire Two: Repentance

Empire Three: Sanctification

Steampunk

The Good, the Bad, and the Ugly: A Readers' and Writers' Guide for Believers

by Sophronia Belle Lyon (pen name for Mary C. Findley)

The Alexander Legacy Steampunk Literary Tribute Series

Book One: A Dodge, a Twist, and a Tobacconist (including illustrated version)

Book Two: The Pinocchio Factor

Book Three: The Most Dangerous Game

Book Four: Beware the Bustle

Fantasy/Allegory

by Mary C. Findley

Allegorical clockwork novella inspired by Little Red Riding Hood

The Acolyte's Education

A Paranormal Urban Fantasy serial

His Sign: The Wait Is Over

His Sign 2: The Ezra Solution

Contemporary Fiction

by Mary C. Findley

Romantic Suspense Novella

Fall On Your Knees

Relationships Short Stories

Fifty Shades of Faithful

Fifty Shades of Faithful 2: In Living Color

The Great Thirst Serial Archaeological Mystery (including boxed set of all titles)

Part One: Prepared

Part Two: Purified

Part Three: Pursued

Part Four: Persecuted

Part Five: Persevering

Part Six: Protected

Part Seven: Prevailing

Murder Mystery

Mapped Out Murders

Nonfiction

by Mary C. Findley

Write for the King of Glory, 2nd Edition (updated, with tips on indie writing and publishing)

by Michael J. and Mary C. Findley

The Good, the Bad, and the Ugly: A Readers' and Writers' Guide for Believers

Biblical Studies (Teacher and student editions plus excerpts in OT and NT Manuscript History)

Antidisestablishmentarianism (illustrated and plain versions)

Serial versions, illustrated and plain

What Is an Establishment of Religion?

What Is Secular Humanism?

What Is Science?

What Are the Results of the Establishment of Secular Humanism?

The Conflict of the Ages series (All have teacher and student editions plus one combined teacher edition for 1-3)

I. The Scientific History of Origins

II. The Origin of Evil in the World that Was

III. They Deliberately Forgot: The Flood and the Ice Age

IV. Ice Age Civilizations

V. The Ancient World

by Michael J. Findley

Short Recaps of longer nonfiction works (*Antidisestablishmentarianism* and *Conflict of the Ages*)

Disestablish: An Overview from Creation to the Ice Age

Under the Sun: The Truth about History from the Beginning

*****

Christian Books in Multiple Genres. Join Christian Indie Author ~ Readers Group on Facebook. https://www.facebook.com/groups/291215317668431/

www.ingramcontent.com/pod-product-compliance
Lightning Source LLC
LaVergne TN
LVHW050552160826
845677LV00011B/2286